EAT CUBAN

EAT CUBAN

**Andy Rose
and
Judy Bastyra**

Photographs by Sam Bailey

SIMON &
SCHUSTER

LONDON • NEW YORK • SYDNEY • TORONTO

First published in Great Britain by Simon & Schuster UK Ltd, 2008
A CBS Company

Simon & Schuster UK Ltd
1st Floor, 222 Gray's Inn Road, London WC1X 8HB

1 3 5 7 9 10 8 6 4 2

Photography: Sam Bailey
Design: Two Associates
Lydia Bell: Consultant
Ben Shipton: Researcher

Printed and bound in China

ISBN 978-1-84737-290-1

SYMBOLS:

♛ Takes under 1 hour

♛ ♛ Takes under 3 hours

♛ ♛ ♛ Takes over 3 hours

Contents

Acknowledgements

My biggest thanks go to my extremely understanding, supportive and wonderful wife, Jenny, and of course my gorgeous step-daughter Amber.

A big thank you to Judy Bastyra, Brian Bendix, Andrew and Ranald McDonald and Max Rhodes whom have supported this project from the start.

Special thanks to Des Gunewardena, David Loewi and Ian Horrox for your support over the years within the company.

This goes without saying – all the team from Floridita London, especially Behar, Flamur and Anis for their loyalty unconditional!

A huge thank you to sponsors Bobby Lea, Peter Way, Alfie Lay, Gillian Pugh, Gabriel Gaya, Floridita London and Carme Farre – without you this would not have been possible.

Many thanks!

Andy Rose

On behalf of Andy and myself, I would like to thank Lydia Bell, Ruth Thomson, Ben Shipton and Angel Coulby for their part in making this book so special. Also to Sally Bourne Interiors for the loan of their props, Sam Bailey for his tireless work and brilliant eye, both in Cuba and here in London. Paula Borton and Janet Copleston – thank you both so much for your positive support whilst producing the book, and thanks also to the designers, David and Kevan of Two Associates. We would also like to say a big thank you to the wonderful people who helped us in Cuba: Robert and his family, Antonio, Mayra, Victor (Cokie) and, last but not least, Alexy.

This is for Dominic and Gaby – I know that this book will not only inspire you in the kitchen but will also inspire you in many other areas of your life. Make sure that you visit Cuba and experience the magic for yourselves.

Judy Bastyra

Sponsors

Floridita London, 100 Wardour Street, London, W1F 0TN
Gaya Ecotrade, 91 Brick Lane, London, E1 6QL
Daily Fish Supplies Ltd, Unit 12–14 Cedar Way Industria, Cedar Way, London, NW1 0PD
Lays of Chelsea, Unit B29–31, New Covent Garden Market, Vauxhall, London, SW8 5HH
Aquila Support Services, Falcon Mews, Oakmead Road, Balham, London SW12 9SJ
Pugh's Piglets, Bowgreave House Farm, Bowgreave, Garstand, Preston, Lancashire, PR3 1YE
Sabor de Espana Ltd, 1 Beachamp Court, Victors Way, Barnet, Herts, London, EN5 5TZ

Cook Cuban

The cuisine of any country cannot be separated from its culture and this is particularly true of Cuban food. Like many other islands in the Caribbean, Cuba is a melting pot of cultures and customs. South American Indians, Spanish, English, Portuguese, African, Arab, Jewish and North Americans have all mixed and mingled with each other to make the distinctive blend of Cuban people today.

Cuba has a unique and delicious cuisine albeit quite difficult to produce at times. It is a cuisine of improvisation. Like its people, it is fiercely traditional yet creative and full of ingenuity. Many of the dishes in Cuba are very simple but each Cuban cook has their own way of adding their special touch to their tried and tested dishes. Truly to appreciate and understand Cuban cuisine, you really have to know about the Cuban way of life.

Writing this book I have taken the foundation of Cuba's traditional cuisine and have put my own spin on it. Although Cuba is geographically in the Caribbean, I discovered that many Cubans feel that they are both Caribbean and Latin American. So, on that basis I have widened my ingredients to include some Latin American produce and imagined how Cuba's cuisine would have developed, had its history taken a different course, enabling a greater variety of ingredients available to its cooks.

One of the most outstanding foods in Cuba is the spiny lobster and it is one of the commodities that I import, whenever I can, live and direct from Cuba. On my most recent visit to Cuba I was astonished at the variety and excellence of the produce that is now available in the markets. There is a huge selection of fresh organic vegetables, fruits and

herbs that are grown locally and the quality and flavour of the free range chicken and pork is second to none. Though still passionate about their traditional dishes, many Cubans are looking at a lighter, healthier cuisine.

Cuban cuisine is most definitely on the cusp of change but these culinary changes are in the most part evolving outside of Cuba.

Floridita London is part of this evolution. Currently other than Floridita, London, Havana Holdings have expanded Floridita to Dublin, Madrid and Moscow with many other exciting destinations on the way.

Enjoy Eat Cuban.

Andy Rose

APPETISERS

Avocado Vinaigrette, Palm Hearts and Orange Salad

Serves 6

3 ripe but firm avocados
juice of 2 lemons
6 tablespoons extra virgin olive oil
1 medium red onion, finely chopped
4 tablespoons red wine vinegar
2 oranges, peeled, pith removed and
    broken into segments
180 g canned palm hearts, drained
    and cut diagonally
6 red radishes, thinly sliced
3 slices of white bread, crusts removed,
    cut into croûtons and shallow fried
    in extra virgin olive oil until crispy
180 g mixed salad leaves
3 tablespoons House Salad Dressing
    (page 120)
salt and freshly ground black pepper
cracked whole black peppercorns,
    to garnish
2 tablespoons finely chopped chives,
    to garnish

Skin and remove the stone from the avocados, cut them into quarters, then thinly slice and fan out on a plate. Spoon over 3 tablespoons of the lemon juice and 2 tablespoons of the olive oil, and season with salt and pepper. Refrigerate until needed. (Note: if the avocados are on the large side, then a quarter avocado per person may be sufficient.)

For the avocado vinaigrette, mix together the red onion, remaining olive oil and lemon juice, vinegar and salt and pepper to taste.

For the salad, toss the orange segments, palm hearts, radishes and croûtons with the mixed salad leaves. Pour over the prepared House Dressing and season with salt and pepper.

To serve, heap some of the salad neatly in the centre of a plate and lay the fanned avocado on top (with the salad below still visible). Pour the vinaigrette over the avocados and drizzle some around the plate. Garnish with the cracked fresh peppercorns and chopped chives.

Stuffed Piquillo Peppers with Soft Cheese and Anchovies

Serves 4

250 g tinned piquillo peppers
    (approximately 12 peppers)
200 g mascarpone cheese
50 g anchovies, chopped
50 g Manchego cheese,
    cut into small cubes
1½ tablespoons fresh chives,
    finely chopped
3 tablespoons freshly grated
    Parmesan cheese
100 g croûtons, shallow fried
    in clarified butter or olive oil
1 tablespoon paprika
100 g mashed potato, prepared
    without butter or milk
2 free range organic egg yolks
salt and freshly ground black pepper

For the garnish
2 handfuls of rocket and frisée
   salad leaves
12 tablespoons Hot Tomato Sauce
   (page 119)
2 tablespoons shaved Parmesan cheese
a drizzle of extra virgin olive oil
1 tablespoon finely chopped fresh chives

Preheat the oven to 180°C/Gas Mark 4.

Rinse the peppers and dry, making sure
they don't break. Mix all the other
ingredients together and season well. Then
use a piping bag with a plain nozzle to fill
the peppers with the mixture. Close the
ends by pushing them down so they meet.

Line a baking sheet with greaseproof
baking paper, then place the stuffed
peppers on top. Warm the peppers through
in the oven for 8 minutes.

To serve, lay a bed of rocket and frisée
salad on each plate. Place three warmed
peppers on top. Spoon over a little warm
Hot Tomato Sauce and drizzle some around.
Sprinkle the shaved Parmesan over the
peppers, drizzle on some olive oil and add a
crack of pepper and chopped chives.

Tuna Tartare, Soft Quails' Eggs and Coriander

Serves 4

400 g fresh tuna, finely chopped
4 spring onions, finely sliced
2 tablespoons light soy sauce
zest and juice of 2 limes
2–3 tablespoons finely chopped
   fresh coriander
50 ml extra virgin olive oil
sea salt and freshly ground black pepper
4 slices of pumpernickel bread
80 g mixed salad leaves
12 quails' eggs, soft-boiled for 3 minutes
a handful of fresh coriander leaves
a drizzle of extra virgin olive oil

For the sour cream dressing
6 tablespoons sour cream
2 tablespoons extra virgin olive oil
juice of 1 lime
1 tablespoon finely chopped fresh chives
salt and freshly ground black pepper

Mix the tuna, spring onions, soy sauce, lime zest
and juice with the coriander and olive oil.
Season. For the sour cream dressing, mix all
the ingredients together and season to taste.

To assemble, cut out a 5 cm circle from the
bread using a round biscuit cutter and
discard the outside. Keeping the bread circle
within the cutter, top with the tuna tartare
then carefully remove the cutter. Divide the
assembled appetisers between four plates
and garnish with the salad leaves and three
quails' eggs each. Pour over the dressing,
decorate with a few coriander leaves and a
drizzle of olive oil.

450 g potatoes, peeled
450 g cooked langouste meat,
   finely chopped
1 tablespoon finely chopped fresh
   flat leaf parsley
1 bunch of spring onions, white parts
   finely chopped
2 free range organic eggs
450 ml vegetable oil, for deep frying
50 g plain flour
100 g dried white breadcrumbs
   (or Japanese 'Panko' breadcrumbs
   if available)
salt and freshly ground black pepper

Cook the potatoes in salted, boiling water for 10–12 minutes. Strain and then mash (without any milk or butter).

Mix the mashed potatoes with the langouste meat, fresh parsley and spring onions. Beat in 1 egg until well mixed. Season with salt and pepper.

Heat the vegetable oil in a deep frying pan to about 180°C/350°F (if you have a thermometer) or until hot but not smoking.

Dip tablespoonfuls of the potato mixture into the flour, then gently shape into sausage shapes with your hands. Beat the remaining egg in a bowl, dip the croquette pieces in the egg mixture and then cover in the breadcrumbs. Deep fry a few at a time for 3–4 minutes, or until golden brown. Remove with a slotted spoon and drain on kitchen paper. Serve at once.

Langosta Croquettas

Makes 8–10

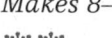

Croquettas (croquettes) are a popular street food in Cuba. They can be filled with a variety of ingredients, from salt fish or prawns, to ham and cheese, or whatever is available. They are sold at little stalls on busy streets and there always seems to be a queue for these tasty delicacies. Cuban langouste (crayfish or spiny lobster) have a succulent, sweet flesh and make a wonderful filling for these delicious snacks.

**Most street food tends to cost just a few pesos –
affordable and a welcome addition to the food rations received
from the government.**

Cubans may not have McDonalds or Kentucky Fried Chicken, but they do have pizza in a basket. Sometimes it is literally delivered in a rattan basket lowered down from an upstairs kitchen, several storeys above the street. The Cubans have a unique way of eating their pizza, folding them over like a calzone and eating them like a sandwich.

Self-employed street vendors hawk paper cones of peanuts, popcorn and a snack known as 'chicharrones de macarones' – fried macaroni and pork rind.

Many street vendors are licensed, and the government runs storefront stands selling pizzas, hot dogs and pork sandwiches for 10 pesos as well as cold 'guarapo' or sugar cane juice for 1 peso. Croquettas and empanadas filled with cheese, ham or fish are also extremely popular and at lunchtime there will be a long queue of people alongside the most coveted stalls.

The longest queue you will find though is outside the futuristic Coppelia ice cream parlour, which is a national institution.

Pickled Mackerel and Mango Escabeche with Herb Salad

Serves 4

'Escabeche' is a traditional Spanish and Portuguese method of cooking fish in a vinegar marinade, and this quick and healthy recipe can be served as a starter or a light lunch dish.

4 x 175 g mackerel fillets, pin-boned
2 heaped tablespoons plain flour
100 ml extra virgin olive oil
2 garlic cloves, crushed
1 red onion, finely chopped
6 tablespoons red wine vinegar
6 tablespoons lime juice
1 jalapeño chilli pepper, de-seeded
    and finely chopped
½ red pepper, de-seeded and
    finely chopped
1 small ripe mango, finely chopped
salt and freshly ground black pepper
baby leaf salad, to serve
2 tablespoons finely chopped fresh
    'fine herbs', such as flat leaf parsley,
    chervil, tarragon and chives, to serve

Dust the mackerel fillets with flour. Heat 2 tablespoons of olive oil in a frying pan and gently fry the fillets over a moderate heat for 2 minutes on each side, or until cooked. Transfer to a plate and set aside while you prepare the escabeche marinade.

Heat the remaining olive oil in a pan, add the garlic and onion, and sweat over a low heat for 5 minutes. Add the red wine vinegar, lime juice, jalapeño chilli pepper and red pepper. Season with salt and pepper, remove from the heat and allow to cool slightly. Then add the mango.

Pour the sauce over the fish and set aside to cool completely before chilling in the fridge for a couple of hours.

Serve the pickled fish with some baby leaf salad, scattering the fresh finely chopped herbs over the fish.

Ropa Vieja of Confit Duck and Jalapeño Crème Fraîche

Serves 4

Traditionally, Ropa Vieja (translated literally it means 'old clothes') is made with skirt or flank of beef that is first stewed, then shredded and cooked again in a rich tomato sauce.

2 duck legs and 2 duck thighs
2 tablespoons salt
100 g melted duck fat to cover
    the duck meat
1 medium onion, finely sliced
2 garlic cloves, crushed
1 green pepper, peeled, de-seeded
    and diced
2 tablespoons extra virgin olive oil
    to fry the vegetables
4 tablespoons sweet sherry
2 plum tomatoes, peeled, de-seeded and
    cut lengthways into 1.5-cm strips
1 tablespoon finely chopped
    fresh parsley
4 free range organic eggs
a dash of cider vinegar
freshly ground black pepper

For the jalapeño crème fraîche
1 teaspoon crushed garlic
100 g shallots, finely chopped
2 tablespoons extra virgin olive oil
2 tablespoons sherry
100 ml chicken stock
100 g crème fraîche
1–2 tablespoons chopped jalapeño chilli
   peppers (according to taste)
1 tablespoon finely chopped
   fresh chives

For the garnish
a large handful of mixed salad leaves
a bunch of fresh chives
fresh cracked black pepper
a drizzle of extra virgin olive oil

First make the confit duck. Rub the duck legs and thighs with the salt and place in the refrigerator.

The next day, preheat the oven to 150°C/ Gas Mark 2. Rinse the salt thoroughly off the duck and pat the duck dry, then place it in a roasting dish. Pour over the duck fat, then cover with tin foil. Slowly cook for 2–2½ hours, or until the meat falls off the bone. Remove the duck from the oven and shred the meat while still warm. Discard the fat, skin and bone.

In a frying pan, sweat the onion, garlic and pepper in a little olive oil over a low heat, until soft. Stir in the sherry, increase the heat to high and reduce the liquid by half. Add the strips of tomato and chopped parsley. Season with black pepper. Remove from the heat and set aside to cool.

Poach the eggs in boiling water and a dash of cider vinegar for 3 minutes, then refresh in iced water.

Now make the crème fraîche. Over a low heat, sweat the garlic and shallots in the olive oil for 5 minutes. Add the sherry, increase the heat to high and boil for a couple of minutes. Add the chicken stock and continue boiling until the liquid has reduced by half.

Stir in the crème fraîche and jalepeño chilli peppers, reduce the heat to moderate and cook until the liquid has, once again, reduced by half. Remove from the heat and set aside to cool. Once cool, stir in the chopped chives.

Mix together the onion mixture with the duck meat, gently warm in a saucepan, then place in a warm bowl.

Divide the duck mixture between four plates. On each plate, lay a well-drained egg on top of the duck and garnish with the mixed salad leaves, the crème fraîche, four long chive batons, fresh cracked pepper and a drizzle of extra virgin olive oil.

Octopus and Squid Escabeche with Spring Onions and Garbanzos

Serves 6

It is always surprising how much an octopus shrinks once it has been cooked. This dish, combining marinated seafood with chickpeas (garbanzos), makes a fantastic appetiser, or it can be served as a light lunch dish with plenty of crunchy hot bread.

1 kg whole octopus, with the
   intestines cleaned
375 ml red wine vinegar
½ teaspoon whole black peppercorns
1 bay leaf
400 g squid, cleaned
100 ml extra virgin olive oil
3 banana shallots, finely diced
2 garlic cloves, crushed
zest and juice zest of 2 lemons
400 g tinned chickpeas, drained
5 spring onions, trimmed and
   finely sliced
400 g tomatoes, skinned, de-seeded
   and cut into large cubes
2 green peppers, peeled, de-seeded
   and diced
salt and freshly ground black pepper
½ bunch roughly chopped fresh
   flat leaf parsley, to serve
mixed salad leaves, to serve
a squeeze of lime juice, to serve

Cover the octopus with water in a large saucepan. Add half the red wine vinegar, black peppercorns and bay leaf. Bring to the boil, skim the surface and then lower the heat. Simmer for 1½ hours, or until tender and soft. The skin and suckers should start to come free. Drain and refresh under cold running water. Set aside until cool, then remove all the skin and suckers, and cut the flesh into 1 cm chunks.

Slice open the squid, score the squid tubes and cut into 1-cm slices. Heat 2 tablespoons of the olive oil in a pan, add the shallots and garlic and sweat over a moderate heat for 5 minutes. Increase the heat to high, add the squid, and sauté for 3–5 minutes, turning constantly. Add the chunks of octopus, lemon zest and juice, then remove from the heat and transfer to a large bowl.

Stir in the chickpeas, spring onions, tomatoes, green peppers, the rest of the red wine vinegar and olive oil to taste. Season well.

To serve, scatter the parsley over the escabeche, then place a portion of this in the middle of a starter plate, reserving the marinade left in the bowl. Arrange the mixed salad leaves around the outside, pour the marinade over the top and add a squeeze of fresh lime.

Red Snapper Ceviche, Coconut and Lime

Serves 4

2 x 125 g fillet of red snapper,
   skinned and boned
zest and juice of 2 limes
2 tablespoons extra virgin olive oil
salt and freshly ground black pepper

For the coconut dressing
125 ml coconut milk
1 tomato, skinned, de-seeded and diced
1 red chilli, de-seeded and chopped
1 small red onion, diced
½ teaspoon hot pepper sauce
   (to taste)

2 tablespoons finely chopped fresh
   coriander leaves
salt and freshly ground black pepper

For the garnish
375 ml vegetable oil for deep frying
½ aubergine, skin peeled and cut into
   very fine julienne strips
4 chicory leaves, shredded
50 g wild rocket
1 teaspoon House Salad Dressing
   (page 120)
a sprinkle of finely chopped
   fresh chives
a drizzle of extra virgin olive oil

Slice the fresh snapper fillets as thinly as possible and arrange on four serving plates.

Drizzle over a dash of fresh lime juice and a little olive oil (reserving the remaining lime zest and juice for the coconut dressing). Lightly season with salt and pepper. Cover with clingfilm and chill in the refrigerator for at least 10 minutes.

To make the coconut dressing, mix together the coconut milk, the rest of the lime zest, juice and olive oil, the tomato, chilli and red onion and season well. To give some heat to the dressing, add the hot pepper sauce (to taste). Chill in the refrigerator for 20 minutes.

Heat about 2.5 cm of the vegetable oil in a deep-sided pan, until hot. Add the aubergine strips and deep fry for a few seconds, until crisp.

To serve, stir the chopped coriander into the coconut dressing, then spoon it over the sliced fish. Dress the chicory and rocket leaves with the house dressing (page 120), then place in the middle of each plate. Scatter over the fried aubergine strips and chopped chives and dress with cracked black pepper and a drizzle of olive oil.

Diver-Caught Scallops, Smoked Eel and Spanish Pancetta with a Purée of Celeriac and Apple and Grain Mustard Salsa

Serves 4

4 rashers of cured Spanish pancetta
200 g hot smoked eel fillet, cut into 4 x
    50 g lengths, leaving the skin on
2 tablespoons of olive oil
8 large diver scallops (ask your
    fishmonger to remove them from
    the shells and clean them free of
    the roe)
salt and freshly ground black pepper

For the celeriac and apple purée
175 g celeriac, peeled and diced
1 Granny Smith apple, peeled and
    cored and diced
1 shallot, finely diced
½ teaspoon minced garlic
1 sprig of thyme
1 bay leaf
2 tablespoons double cream

For the grain mustard salsa
1 teaspoon grain mustard
1 tablespoon lime juice
1 tablespoon white wine vinegar
1 tablespoon extra virgin olive oil
1 teaspoon finely diced tomatoes
1 teaspoon finely diced shallots
1 teaspoon finely chopped chives
salt and freshly ground black pepper,
    to taste

Preheat the oven to 170°C/Gas Mark 3.

First of all, make the celeriac and apple purée. Put the celeriac, apple, shallot, garlic, thyme and bay leaf in a saucepan. Cover with water and bring to the boil. Simmer for 10 minutes, or until the celeriac is soft. Strain well. Blitz with a hand-held blender and stir in the cream. Season and keep warm.

Using a fork, mix the mustard, lime juice and white wine vinegar together. Continue mixing while slowly pouring in the olive oil. Add the other ingredients, season and reserve.

Cover a baking tray with parchment paper and place the rashers of pancetta on top. Place another sheet of parchment paper over the top and sandwich with another baking tray. Place in the oven for 15–20 minutes or until crispy. Remove and leave in a warm place.

Meanwhile, peel back the skin of the eel halfway widthways and tuck the loose end under itself. Place on a tray and slowly warm through in the preheated oven.

Place a frying pan over a hot heat, add a little oil and heat until it starts to smoke. Season the scallops, then pan fry for 30 seconds to 1 minute on each side, depending on how thick they are, or until they are caramelized and golden brown on both sides. Remove from the pan and allow to rest.

Put a spoonful of purée on each plate. Place two scallops and a portion of the eel on top, drizzle over some of the salsa, rest the pancetta on top and serve.

Oven-Baked Tortilla

Makes 24 bite-size tortillas

10 g softened butter
2 tablespoons extra virgin olive oil
1 large garlic clove, crushed
4 spring onions, both green and white parts chopped
1 green pepper, de-seeded and finely diced
1 fresh red pepper, de-seeded and finely diced
375 g potatoes, peeled, diced and shallow-fried in olive oil until soft
5 free range organic eggs
100 g crème fraîche
4 tablespoons chopped fresh chives
300 g freshly grated Manchego cheese
salt and freshly ground black pepper

Preheat the oven to 180°C/Gas Mark 4.

Grease a deep 25 x 22 cm ovenproof dish with the butter, then line with a piece of greaseproof paper, making sure that it's pushed well into the edges and corners of the tray.

Heat the olive oil in a saucepan over a low heat, add the garlic, spring onions and pepper and sweat for 6–8 minutes, until soft but without colour. Leave to cool slightly and then stir in the cooked potatoes.

Beat together the eggs, crème fraîche, chives and Manchego cheese. Stir in the softened vegetables and season well. Pour the mixture into the baking tray, knocking it several times on the tabletop to level the top.

Bake in the oven for 40–50 minutes until golden brown, slightly risen and set. (Use a knife to test this.) Remove from the oven and set aside to cool.

Turn the tortilla out on a chopping board, keeping the coloured side up. Slice into bite-size pieces and serve.

'Havana has the ramshackle glamour of an abandoned stage set'

PICO LYER, WRITER

The desiccated beauty and ruined facades of Havana's humid streets, its amusing hustlers and its sultry beats make it hard not to romanticize the city. Impossibly cool cars cruise the streets; beautiful faces look out of bars and gaze from balconies; gorgeous, laughing children throw themselves into the water from the Malecon sea wall and couples in love entwine in the dusk. Even the political slogans have an undeniable poetry: *La moral de la revolución esta tan alta como las estrellas* ('the future of the revolution is written in the stars'). Even the hardest heart cannot fail to conclude that the sensual exotica of Cuba must surely make up for the challenges of living a Cuban life.

SOUPS
AND SALADS

Black Bean and Coconut Soup

Serves 6

Black beans are one of the staple ingredients in Cuban food. This version of black bean soup uses coconut milk, which gives it a rich and creamy flavour. Although hot peppers are not used much in Cuban cooking, I have spiced up the dish with a touch of Scotch Bonnet hot pepper. Culantro, a herb with an assertive sage-citrus flavour native to Latin America is used for making soups and sauces, but if you can't find it, use coriander instead.

450 g black beans
100 g whole piece of pancetta
4 garlic cloves, peeled, 2 cloves left
   whole and 2 cloves crushed
2 onions, peeled, 1 onion cut in half
   and 1 onion finely chopped
1 carrot
1 bay leaf
2 sprigs of culantro (or small bunch
   of fresh coriander)
2 tablespoons extra virgin olive oil
2 tomatoes, skinned, de-seeded
   and chopped
1 x 400 g tin coconut milk
3 tablespoons finely chopped
   fresh coriander
1 Scotch Bonnet hot pepper, left whole
3 tablespoons crème fraîche
salt and freshly ground black pepper

Put the black beans, pancetta, whole garlic cloves, onion halves, carrot, bay leaf and culantro in a large saucepan. Pour in 1 litre of water and bring to the boil. Reduce the heat to low, simmer for 1½–2 hours, or until the beans are tender. Strain and discard the flavouring ingredients, put the beans aside and reserve the cooking liquor.

Heat the oil in a saucepan, add the chopped onion and crushed garlic and cook for 10 minutes over a low heat. Add the tomatoes and cook for a further 3 minutes.

Add four-fifths of the black beans to the pan and pour in 600 ml of the cooking liquid and the tin of coconut milk. Add 1 tablespoon of the chopped coriander and the Scotch Bonnet hot pepper. Season with salt and pepper.

Bring the soup to the boil, then lower the heat and simmer for 20 minutes. Remove from the heat, allow to cool slightly, then remove the Scotch Bonnet hot pepper. Blend the soup with a hand-held blender or in a liquidizer to a rough purée. Add the remaining beans.

Serve with a swirl of crème fraîche and the rest of the chopped coriander.

Grilled Swordfish, Shaved Fennel and Pink Grapefruit Salad

Serves 4

1 bulb of fennel
4 x 180 g swordfish steaks
2 tablespoons extra virgin olive oil
1 medium red onion, thinly sliced
1 ruby pink grapefruit, cut in half
   and segmented
20 g fresh coriander leaves
zest and juice of 2 limes
salt and freshly ground black pepper
2 limes, cut in half, to garnish

With a Chinese mandolin or a very sharp knife, slice the fennel lengthways into wafer-thin slices and place in iced water.

Season the swordfish and brush on 1 tablespoon of the olive oil. Place the steaks on a grill and grill for 2 minutes on each side over a moderate to high heat. Remove from the heat and leave to rest for a further 4 minutes in a warm place.

Remove the fennel from the water and drain well. Toss with the red onion, grapefruit, coriander, lime zest and juice and the remaining olive oil. Season with salt and pepper.

To serve, divide the salad amongst four plates. Slice the swordfish and lay it over the top. Garnish with the fresh lime halves.

Chicken Liver Salad, Spinach, Bacon and Croûtons

Serves 4

400 g ciabatta bread, crusts
   removed and cut into 2 cm cubes
8 tablespoons extra virgin olive oil
200 g streaky bacon, sliced
450 g fresh chicken livers, cleaned
1 teaspoon ground allspice
320 g baby spinach leaves
1 medium red onion, sliced
2 tablespoons white wine vinegar
2–4 tablespoons balsamic vinegar
salt and freshly ground black pepper

Preheat the oven to 180°C/Gas Mark 4. In a bowl, toss the bread cubes with 2 tablespoons of the olive oil. Place on a baking sheet and bake for about 15 minutes, stirring once or twice, until golden brown. Leave the croûtons to cool.

Heat a non-stick frying pan over a medium heat, add the bacon and cook until crisp. Remove and drain off any fat. Wipe out the pan and heat 2 tablespoons of the olive oil over a medium heat. Season the chicken livers with the allspice, salt and pepper, then fry in batches for 2 minutes on each side, until golden but still pink. Remove from the heat and leave to rest in a warm place.

In a large bowl, mix the baby spinach leaves with the red onion, then add the croûtons, bacon and vinegars. Warm the remaining olive oil in a pan and pour it over the spinach leaves. Toss well, season to taste and serve.

Cream of Sweetcorn Bisque, Tiger Prawns and Coriander Butter

Serves 8

This is the perfect soup for pescatarians (people who don't eat meat but eat fish). It is made with both a fish and prawn stock but, if you're cooking for carnivores, you can use a chicken stock instead of the fish stock.

500 g tiger prawns with shells
150 ml white wine
1 bay leaf
30 g butter
100 g shallots, chopped
6 garlic cloves, crushed
60 g fennel, chopped
500 g frozen sweetcorn, defrosted
300 ml double cream
2 tablespoons extra virgin olive oil
salt and freshly ground black pepper

For the coriander butter
1 green chilli, de-seeded and
    finely chopped
½ teaspoon sea salt
½ teaspoon freshly ground
    black pepper
125 g butter
2 tablespoons finely chopped
    fresh coriander

For the garnish
6 slices of white baguette, toasted
1 teaspoon fresh oregano leaves,
    chopped
2 red chillies, de-seeded and chopped

First make the shellfish stock. Peel the prawns and put the shells and heads (if supplied) in a pan with the white wine, bay leaf and about 1 litre of water. Bring to the boil, skim the surface and reduce the heat to low. Simmer for 30 minutes or until the stock has reduced to 850 ml.

While the stock is reducing, cut through the backs of the prawns and remove the intestines.

To make the coriander butter, mix all the ingredients together until well blended and use as desired (you can freeze the remainder).

To finish making the soup, melt the butter in a saucepan, add the shallots and garlic and sweat over a low heat for 5 minutes, until soft. Add the fennel and sweetcorn, and continue to cook for 2–3 minutes. Strain in the shellfish stock and bring to the boil. Reduce the heat to low and simmer for 3 minutes.

Remove the soup from the heat, pour it into a liquidiser and blitz. Pour it back into the pan through a sieve or chinoise. Stir in the cream, place the pan over a low heat and season well.

In a non-stick frying pan, heat the olive oil and flash-fry the prawns for half a minute or so. Remove the pan from the heat, set it aside until the prawns are cool enough to handle, then cut each prawn in half.

To serve, place six half prawns in the bottom of a warmed soup bowl, pour over the hot soup, float the toasted baguette croûton on top (spread with a slice of coriander butter) and sprinkle over the oregano and chilli.

Chilled Gazpacho Soup with Salsa Cruda and Croûtons

Serves 6

1 kg tomatoes, peeled, de-seeded
   and chopped
1 green pepper, de-seeded and chopped
1 cucumber, peeled, de-seeded
   and chopped
1 free range organic egg,
   hard-boiled and shell removed
12 slices of white bread, crusts
   removed and soaked in 375 ml
   tomato juice
1 onion, chopped
1 garlic clove, crushed
200 g tomato ketchup
1 teaspoon sugar
1 tablespoon smoked paprika
300 ml extra virgin olive oil,
   plus a little more for drizzling
4 tablespoons red wine vinegar
salt and freshly ground black pepper,
   to taste

For the salsa cruda
2 tomatoes, peeled, de-seeded
   and diced
½ green pepper, de-seeded and diced
¼ cucumber, peeled, de-seeded
   and diced
½ red onion, diced

For the garnish
6 tablespoons croûtons
2 tablespoons toasted almonds
olive oil

Blitz the soup ingredients in a food processor. Pour into a bowl and chill in the refrigerator for 30 minutes.

Combine all the ingredients for the salsa cruda in a bowl. Serve the gazpacho in individual bowls, garnished with the salsa cruda, croûtons, toasted almonds and a drizzle of olive oil.

Langosta Salad with Mango and Papaya Salsa

Serves 4

Cuba is renowned for its langosta, a spiny lobster or crayfish that boasts a succulent meat and sweet flavour. Lobster farming has played a vital role in the Cuban economy, the key to its success being cooperation rather than competition among fishermen. This is made workable by exclusive fishing zones and fleet organisation.

2 x 600 g langosta (crayfish or spiny
   lobster), pre-poached, halved

For the mango and papaya salsa
1 mango, peeled, stoned and diced
1 small papaya, pceled, de-seeded
   and diced
2 medium red onions, finely diced
1 spring onion, finely sliced
200 g plum tomatoes, skinned,
   de-seeded and diced
zest and juice of 2 limes
2 tablespoons red wine vinegar
1 mild red chilli, de-seeded and
   finely sliced
2½ tablespoons extra virgin olive oil
salt and freshly ground black pepper

For the garnish
4 tablespoons cold mashed potatoes
75 g mixed salad leaves
2 tablespoons finely chopped
   fresh coriander

Remove the meat from the langosta
(lobster) shells and cut into 2 cm cubes.
Transfer the diced langosta to a bowl and
then make the mango and papaya salsa.

Combine the mango, papaya, red onion,
spring onion, tomatoes, lime zest and juice,
red wine vinegar, chilli and olive oil
together in a mixing bowl. Transfer 4
tablespoons of the mixture to a little bowl,
and then gently fold the diced lobster meat
into the remaining mixture. Season well.
Divide the langosta mixture between the
four shells.

To assemble, place a spoonful of the mashed
potato in the centre of each plate to hold
the langosta in place. Place the langosta
shells on top. Pile some salad leaves in the
centre of the langosta and dress with the
reserved salsa. Add a drizzle of olive oil and
sprinkle over the coriander leaves.

Red Bean, Ham and Garlic Caldo with Chicken Meatballs

Serves 6

250 g red kidney beans, soaked overnight
1 bay leaf
450 g unsmoked ham hock
400 g potatoes, peeled and diced
2 tablespoons extra virgin olive oil
1 large onion, chopped
1 green pepper, diced
3 garlic cloves, crushed
2 x 400 g tin tomatoes
1 tablespoon tomato purée
100 g Savoy cabbage, shredded
salt and freshly ground black pepper
good quality olive oil, for drizzling
2 tablespoons finely chopped fresh
    parsley, to garnish

For the chicken meatballs
1 teaspoon cumin seeds
225 g minced chicken
½ slice white bread, crusts removed
    and chopped
1 tablespoon beer
1 teaspoon finely chopped fresh chives
1 teaspoon finely chopped
    fresh coriander
1 garlic clove, crushed
1 free range organic egg white
2 tablespoons flour, for flouring
sunflower oil, for frying

Place the beans in a pot, add the bay leaf
and ham hock, and cover with water. Bring
to the boil, lower the heat and simmer for 3
hours. Skim the surface at regular intervals.

While the bean and ham soup is cooking,
make the chicken meatballs. Toast the cumin
seeds in a dry non-stick frying pan over a low
heat for 2–3 minutes, stirring constantly
with a wooden spoon. Remove from the heat,
grind the seeds in a coffee grinder and then
mix into the minced chicken.

Soak the bread in the beer and add to the
minced chicken with the chives, coriander
and garlic. Add the egg white and mix well
together. Season with salt and pepper.
Sprinkle the flour over a work surface.
Break off about a teaspoonful of the
mixture at a time and roll into balls on the
floured work surface.

Heat a large frying pan over a moderate heat,
add the sunflower oil and fry the chicken
meatballs for 4–6 minutes, or until golden
brown. Keep warm while you finish the soup.

Add the potatoes to the soup and cook for a
further 30 minutes. Meanwhile, heat the olive
oil in a non-stick frying pan, add the onion,
pepper and garlic and sweat for 5 minutes.
Stir in the tomatoes and the tomato purée,
and cook for 10 minutes. Add to the soup.

Remove the bay leaf and ham from the
soup, and set the ham aside for a few
minutes, until it is cool enough to handle.
Remove the meat from the bone – it should
just fall off – and slice into 1 cm chunks.
Season to taste with salt and pepper.

To serve, spoon the soup into six bowls
with the hot meatballs, slices of ham and
shredded cabbage. Drizzle with a little olive
oil and some freshly chopped parsley.

Chayote, Pumpkin and Pineapple Salad with Mint Dressing

Serves 6

Chayote is a member of the pumpkin family, and with its crisp texure and delicate flavour it offers a delicious alternative to staple salad ingredients. Hot and cold, sweet and sour, spicy and crunchy – this unusual combination of ingredients makes a very interesting dish.

2 raw chayotes, peeled, cored and cubed
450 g pumpkin, peeled, cored and cubed
1 bay leaf
2 cinnamon sticks
½ teaspoon salt
3 tablespoons brown sugar
¼ teaspoon ground allspice
½ teaspoon finely chopped red chilli
½ pineapple, peeled, cored and cubed
mixed salad leaves
3 tablespoons pumpkin seeds, roasted
2 tablespoons torn fresh mint leaves

For the dressing
2 garlic cloves, crushed
4 tablespoons cider vinegar
4 tablespoons extra virgin olive oil
a pinch of ground allspice
1 tablespoon white sugar
½ teaspoon finely chopped red chilli
salt and freshly ground black pepper
1 tablespoon finely chopped fresh mint

First make the dressing. Whisk together all the ingredients in a large mixing bowl. Add the chayote cubes and set aside.

Put the pumpkin pieces in a saucepan, add the bay leaf and cinnamon sticks, and cover with water. Add the salt and bring to the boil over a moderate heat. Cook for 8–10 minutes, or until tender but not too soft. Drain and dry thoroughly on kitchen paper. Transfer the pumpkin to the mixing bowl and gently toss with the chayote, ensuring that everything is coated with the dressing.

In a large frying pan, dissolve the sugar with 2 tablespoons of water. Stir in the allspice and chopped chilli. When the mixture begins to caramelize, add the pineapple cubes and heat through for 2–3 minutes, stirring constantly, to ensure that the cubes are coated with the mixture.

Stir the pineapple cubes into the chayote and pumpkin. Add the salad leaves and lightly toss the ingredients together. Garnish with the roasted pumpkin seeds and fresh mint leaves.

Caesar Salad

Serves 4

1 large Romaine lettuce,
   washed, dried and chopped

For the dressing
1 garlic clove, crushed
2 free range organic egg yolks
2 good quality anchovies,
   finely chopped
100 ml sherry vinegar
2 heaped tablespoons freshly grated
   Parmesan cheese
3 drops of Worcestershire sauce
200 ml extra virgin olive oil
salt and freshly ground black pepper

For the garnish
4 mini flutes (small thin baguette),
   sliced
sunflower oil, for frying
2 tablespoons freshly shaved
   Parmesan cheese
1 tablespoon finely chopped fresh chives
4 good quality anchovies

To make the dressing, whisk the garlic, egg yolks, anchovies, sherry vinegar, Parmesan cheese and Worcestershire sauce together until thoroughly blended. Slowly whisk in the olive oil. Season to taste with salt and pepper. Fry the mini flutes in a little oil to make croûtons.

Toss the salad with the dressing and croûtons. Serve with the Parmesan shavings, chives and 1 anchovy fillet on each plate.

City farming is a remarkable success story

In Cuba, the urban garden (organoponicos) emerged as a practical way of getting food into people's mouths when there was no petrol to transport food.

It has now become a role model for the world in the practice of organic agriculture as most of the food is eaten where it is grown – inside cities.

City farming is a remarkable success story. It produces a startling 60 per cent of Cuba's vegetables. Indeed vegetable stalls are prevalent on many pavements and street corners. Every nook and cranny is utilised to grow a vast array of produce. Over a million patios and private urban plots are registered and all benefit from tremendous official support.

Beef Carpaccio, Plantain and Potato Salad on a Bed of Rocket

Serves 6

375 g beef fillet, trimmed of fat
50 g coriander seeds, crushed
4 tablespoons extra virgin olive oil
4 tablespoons coarse grain mustard
4 tablespoons finely chopped
   fresh coriander
375 g potatoes, diced
1 sweet plantain, diced
salt and freshly ground black pepper
125 g rocket, to garnish
50 g shaved Manchego cheese,
   to garnish

For the red onion dressing
½ small red onion, finely chopped
2 garlic cloves
3 tablespoons olive oil
juice of ½ a lime

For the simple dressing
3 tablespoons olive oil
1 tablespoon balsamic vinegar
salt and freshly ground black pepper

Season the beef fillet well with salt and pepper. Dust with the crushed coriander seeds.

Heat 1 tablespoon of olive oil in a large pan and, when smoking, add the fillet and cook for 5 minutes, turning several times to seal it, until it is a light golden brown.

Transfer the beef to a plate and set aside to cool. When cool, roll the fillet in the mustard and then in 2 tablespoons of the chopped coriander. Wrap in clingfilm and freeze for 1 hour.

Make the red onion dressing: mix all the ingredients together until thoroughly combined.

Cook the potatoes and plantain separately in salted water for approximately 6 minutes, or until tender. Drain and, whilst still warm, toss in the red onion dressing. Season with salt and pepper. Add the remaining coriander, cover and keep warm.

Now make the simple dressing by mixing all the ingredients together.

Using a slicing machine or a very sharp knife, slice the beef very finely directly on to each plate. Leave a well in the centre. Drizzle some of the simple dressing over the meat and season with salt and black pepper. Garnish with the wild rocket and shaved Manchego cheese. Then pile some of the warm potato and plantain salad into the middle.

The Cuban architectural landscape, reflecting half a millennium of history, is a scene of ravaged Spanish colonial buildings – baroque and neo-classical – spattered with art deco and art nouveau apartment blocks and public buildings, and the occasional Soviet monstrosity. Much of its capital is in a vast dilapidated state, particularly in working-class central Havana, because no one had the money to save their beautiful ruins from the ravages of the sun, hurricanes and tropical rain. Towns beyond Havana remain remarkably unspoilt and intact because of Cuba's isolation. One gets the feeling that, even if buildings are neglected and hanging by a thread, at least they are not destroyed.

There is an incredible architectural consistency to its beautiful rhythmic arcades, constructed by Spanish immigrants with Andalusia in mind

FISH
AND SHELLFISH

Salt Cod Stew with Olives and Tomatoes

Serves 4

500 g salt cod fillet, soaked in cold water
for 2 hours, then water refreshed
and soaked overnight
225 g sweet potatoes, peeled and diced
3 tablespoons extra virgin olive oil
1 large onion, finely sliced
1 banana shallot, sliced
4 garlic cloves, chopped
1 teaspoon de-seeded and finely chopped
chilli (optional)
2 x 400 g tin plum tomatoes, chopped
1 x 400 g tin coconut milk
4 tablespoons finely chopped fresh
coriander leaves
4 tablespoons finely chopped fresh
parsley leaves
30 small black stoned olives
salt and freshly ground black pepper

Drain the salt cod, cover with fresh water, bring to the boil and then discard the water. Cover the salt cod with fresh cold water, bring back to the boil and boil for 5 minutes. Drain. Let the fish cool and cut into chunks.

Cook the sweet potatoes in boiling water for 8 minutes until tender, then drain and reserve. In a large pan, add the olive oil and sauté the onion and shallot for 6–8 minutes, or until golden brown. Stir in the garlic, chilli (if using) and the plum tomatoes. Bring to the boil and simmer for 5 minutes.

Pour in the coconut milk, season with salt and pepper, add half the coriander and half the parsley and bring back to the boil. Lower the heat and add the salt cod pieces and the sweet potatoes. Cook for 10 minutes. Add the olives and cook for a further 5 minutes.

Remove from the heat, stir in the remaining coriander and parsley. Serve with some plain white rice and a green salad.

Seared Tuna on a Tomato and Bread Salad

Serves 4

200 g tuna steaks

375 g ripe plum tomatoes, peeled and
  cut into 1 cm wedges

175 g cucumbers, peeled, de-seeded
  and cubed

2 tablespoons chopped fresh
  basil leaves

1 teaspoon chopped fresh
  oregano leaves

2 tablespoons extra virgin olive oil, plus
  extra for frying

½ red onion, diced

2 tablespoons balsamic vinegar

12 stoned Kalamata olives

3 slices of ciabatta bread, cut into
  5 mm cubes and baked in the oven
  to make croûtons

sea salt and freshly ground
  black pepper

For the marinade

3 tablespoons lemon juice

1 sprig of fresh thyme

2 sprigs of fresh rosemary, broken in half

2 garlic cloves

4 tablespoons olive oil

2 tablespoons balsamic vinegar

salt and freshly ground black pepper

First make the marinade. In a large shallow bowl, whisk together the lemon juice, thyme, rosemary, garlic, olive oil and balsamic vinegar. Season with salt and pepper. Add the tuna steaks, turning them several times, and leave to marinate for

approximately 30 minutes, but no longer than 2 hours.

Mix together the tomatoes, cucumbers, basil, oregano, olive oil, red onion, balsalmic vinegar, olives and the croûtons. Divide amongst four serving plates and set aside for 30 minutes.

Meanwhile, lightly brush a non-stick frying pan or griddle with some olive oil and place over a high heat. When hot, sear the tuna on each side for 1 minute. Remove from the heat and transfer the tuna to a cutting board. Slice each steak into 1 cm strips and arrange on top of the salad.

Paella Creole

Serves 6–8

Spanish influence still prevails in Cuban
cooking through the use of onions, tomatoes,
garlic and European herbs. In Havana there
are several restaurants that are solely
dedicated to making paella.

2 tablespoons extra virgin olive oil
2 banana shallots, finely chopped
2 garlic cloves, crushed
4 spring onions, finely chopped
125 g chorizo, diced

225 g tomatoes, de-seeded and chopped
1 teaspoon saffron powder,
    dissolved in 2 tablespoons water
1 teaspoon finely chopped
    jalapeño chilli pepper
375 ml white wine
450 g baby octopus, cleaned
1 whole Scotch Bonnet hot pepper
450 g small mussels or clams,
    scrubbed and de-bearded
600 g langouste tails, cut into sections
450 g stone crabs claws, cracked
450 g paella rice
375 ml coconut milk
150 ml chicken or fish stock

125 g frozen green peas, left to defrost
1 tablespoon finely chopped
   fresh coriander
1 tablespoon finely chopped
   fresh parsley
salt and freshly ground black pepper

For the black beans
250 g black beans, soaked overnight
1 sprig of fresh thyme
125 g chorizo sausage, in one piece
1 onion, halved
1 carrot
1 celery stick
1 bay leaf
salt and freshly ground black pepper

First prepare the beans. Drain and rinse the black beans and transfer to a large saucepan with a tight-fitting lid. Add the thyme, chorizo, onion, carrot, celery stick and bay leaf. Pour over enough water to cover. Season with salt and pepper. Place the lid on and boil rapidly for 10 minutes, then reduce the heat and cook for about 1½ hours, adding more water if needed.

Meanwhile, half an hour before the beans are cooked, heat the olive oil in a large deep-sided frying pan, casserole or paella dish and add the shallots, garlic and spring onion. Reduce the heat to low, cover the pan and sweat for 5 minutes, until soft. Stir in the diced chorizo and tomatoes and cook for a further 5 minutes. Season and add the saffron and jalapeño chilli pepper.

Pour over the white wine and bring to the boil. Lower the heat to moderate, add the whole octopus and Scotch Bonnet hot pepper, and cook for 15 minutes. Stir in the mussels or clams, the langouste tails, crab and rice. Pour over the coconut milk and stock, and cook for a further 20 minutes.

Drain the cooked beans and discard the seasoning. Stir the beans and raw peas into the seafood mixture and cook for a further 5 minutes, until heated through. Remove the Scotch Bonnet hot pepper. Stir in the coriander and parsley and serve immediately.

Langosta/Lobster Thermidor

Serves 2

El Floridita in Havana is renowned for its Lobster Thermidor. This classic French dish illustrates the haute cuisine influences in Cuban food prior to the Revolution in 1959, when Cuba was a playground for the rich.

2 x 625 g langouste, pre-poached
  (alternatively, use 2 x 750 g
  pre-poached lobsters)
50 g butter
I banana shallot, finely chopped
2 tablespoons of white wine
8 tablespoons Béchamel Sauce (page 122)
125 g button mushrooms,
  cut into quarters
2 tablespoons freshly grated
  Parmesan cheese
3 limes, cut in half, to garnish
salt and freshly ground black pepper

Preheat the oven to 180°C/Gas Mark 4 and turn on the grill to high.

Remove the pre-poached lobster or langouste from the shell and cut into large chunks. Wash and dry the shells and reserve until needed.

In a covered saucepan, melt 2 tablespoons of the butter over a low heat, add the shallots and sweat for 3–5 minutes, until soft. Add the lobster meat and sauté for 3 minutes over a moderate heat. Stir in a splash of the white wine, then fold in the

Grilled Marlin, Crushed New Potatoes, Cured Ham and Clam Salsa

Serves 4

180 g new potatoes, scrubbed clean
100 ml extra virgin olive oil
40 g Parma (or similar Spanish)
    cured ham, diced
8 x 80 g medallion of marlin loin or
    4 x 160 g marlin steaks
zest and juice of 2 limes
1 medium onion, finely diced
20 g fresh flat leaf parsley,
    finely chopped
500 g clams, washed and steamed,
    removed from shells
salt and freshly ground black pepper
a handful of fresh flat leaf parsley,
    to garnish
2 limes cut in half, to garnish

Béchamel Sauce. Remove from the heat and set aside.

Put the lobster shells in the oven to heat through for a few minutes.

Meanwhile, melt the remaining butter in a frying pan, add the mushrooms and cook over a moderate heat for 3–4 minutes. Add the remaining white wine, season with salt and pepper and cook for a further minute.

Remove the warmed lobster shells from the oven and fill them first with the mushrooms, followed by the lobster mixture. Sprinkle with the Parmesan cheese and bake under the grill for 3–4 minutes, or until golden brown. Garnish with the lime halves.

Boil the potatoes until tender. Drain and crush with the back of a fork. Season. Heat 1 tablespoon of olive oil in a small frying pan, add the ham and fry for 2 minutes. Fold into the potatoes and put aside.

Heat the grill to high. Season the marlin, brush with olive oil and grill for 2 minutes on each side. Reserve in a warm place.

Put the rest of the olive oil, lime zest and juice, onion, parsley and clams in a saucepan and warm for 2 minutes (don't boil).

To serve, place some of the potatoes on a plate, lay over the grilled marlin and coat with plenty of the clam salsa. Garnish with the fresh parsley and lime halves.

Cuba: Pre revolution

Spotted by Christopher Columbus in 1492, circumnavigated by the conquistadores in 1509, first colonized from 1510, Cuba was ruled for 400 years (apart from a short break under the British in the late 1800s) by Spain. Spain grew fat on the profits of sugar cane, importing 600,000 slaves

> '**The echo of the slow swelling pulse of the dance music, and the glorious intonation of the Spanish speech, the odour of a thousand orange blossoms.**'
>
> MRS SHERWOOD, *New York Times*

between 1800 and 1865 to support this industry. The Spanish made covetable Havana into the most fortified city in the Americas and presided over a highly stratified society, consisting of a Spanish and Creole ruling class of tobacco, sugar and coffee plantation owners, a middle class of black and Spanish workers and an underclass of black slaves.

The island gained independence in the Spanish-American war of 1898, and the 20th century began under American influence. Havana grew and prospered – swish mansions, casinos, luxury hotels and clubs characterized Havana between the 1930s and the 1960s, but this came at a price. Fulgencio Batista (left) controlled Cuba on and off from about 1934 onwards (finally seizing power in a 1952 coup). Helped by the prohibition in the United States, he aligned himself with US big business and organized crime, and made Cuba a mecca for fast living.

At the Hotel Nacional, black and white pictures remain of Frank Sinatra, Ava Gardner, Marlene Dietrich and Gary Cooper. American tourists cavorted everywhere. Writers were attracted to Cuba, intoxicated by the city's beauty and licentiousness, immortalized in the novels of Hemingway (seen above with Fidel Castro) and Graham Greene. Meanwhile, the rest of desperately poor agricultural Cuba slaved in the fields. When Batista fled Cuba in 1959, the elite followed, leaving behind cars, mansions, and objets d'art. All were seized by the Revolutionaries.

Chilean Sea Bass with Shrimps and Clams in a Beurre Blanc Sauce

Serves 4

4 x150 g fillets Chilean sea bass
2 tablespoons butter
125 g large shrimps

400 g palourde clams, cleaned and
 steamed
225 ml white wine
a few parsley stalks
Beurre Blanc (page 117)
400 g fresh spinach leaves, steamed
salt and freshly ground black pepper
2 tablespoons finely chopped fresh dill,
 to garnish

Preheat the oven to 180°C/Gas Mark 4. Season the sea bass with salt and pepper and half of the butter, then place on a roasting tray and gently roast in the oven for 12 minutes, depending on the thickness.

Poach the clams lightly with the white wine and parsley stalks for about 6 minutes. Remove from the heat and allow to cool slightly, then remove the shells. Add the shellfish to the Beurre Blanc. Toss the steamed spinach in the remaining butter.

To serve, divide the spinach between four plates and place the roasted sea bass on top. Spoon over the Beurre Blanc and shellfish. Garnish with dill.

Creole-Spiced Red Snapper with Olive Sofrito

Serves 6

6 x 175 g fillet of red snapper, scaled and
　pin-boned (red mullet would make a
　good alternative)
extra virgin olive oil
3 limes, cut in half

For the olive sofrito
75 g unsalted butter
3 garlic cloves, thinly sliced
1 large onion, finely chopped
1 large courgette, cut into 1 cm cubes
1 teaspoon capers
3 tablespoons stoned Kalamata olives,
　finely chopped
6 plum tomatoes, peeled, de-seeded
　and quartered
zest and juice of 1 lime
2 tablespoons finely chopped fresh
　coriander leaves
salt and freshly ground black pepper

For the spice rub
1 teaspoon ground cumin
½ teaspoon salt
1 teaspoon cayenne pepper
½ teaspoon finely ground white pepper
1 teaspoon paprika
1 teaspoon fresh oregano,
　finely chopped

First make the sofrito. Heat the butter in a pan, add the garlic and onion and sweat for 5–8 minutes over a low heat, until soft. Add the courgette, capers and olives, and cook for 5 minutes over a moderate heat until the courgette cubes are cooked but still firm. Cool and set aside.

For the spice rub, mix the ground cumin, salt, cayenne pepper, white pepper, paprika and oregano in a bowl. Brush both sides of the fish fillets with olive oil. Sprinkle half of the spice rub on a tray, then lay the fillets on top, pressing down gently. Sprinkle over the remaining spice rub and press into the fillets. Turn to make sure that they are evenly coated.

Heat a heavy frying pan over a hot heat for a few minutes, then add the snapper fillets skin-side down. Cook for 2½–3 minutes, then turn and fry for 1 minute before serving. (The precise cooking time will depend on the thickness of the fillets.)

To finish the sofrito, heat a tablespoon of olive oil in a hot pan, add the tomatoes, followed by the olive mixture, and cook for a few minutes. Remove from the heat, stir in the lime zest, juice of 1 lime and coriander leaves and season to taste.

To serve, divide the sofrito between six plates and pile the snapper fillets on top. Finish with a drizzle of extra virgin olive oil, the juice of half a lime each and a grind of fresh black pepper. Accompany with a crisp green salad.

On 2 January 1959, Che Guevara and Camilo Cienfuegos led their rebel army in Havana as Fidel Castro approached to join them across the island, ushering in El Trionfo de la Revolución

Moscow cleverly stepped in, offering the lifeblood of food and oil subsidies in return for missile bases on the island. The 1960s were characterized by nationalisation, industrialisation, the exodus of skilled workers and rationing (which continues today). As huge USSR subsidies boosted Cuba, there was an improvement in the 1970s. By the 1980s, when Castro allowed free emigration from the port of Mariel, 125,000 Cubans left. At the end of the Cold War more than 80 per cent of the country's trade disappeared overnight and the resulting shortages were crippling. After the USSR collapsed, the imperialist dollar was once again banned, and Castro introduced the CUC, the convertible currency to stay away from the US. By the 1990s, the worst was over as the island threw its doors open to foreign tourists.

The CUC, used by tourists and foreign businessmen, is worth about the same as an American dollar, whereas the Cuban peso is worth just about four US cents. The average Cuban salary is about 400 pesos a month, which is approximately $15. The question of dual currency is said to be high on the list of items for the new government to review.

Castro finally retired in February 2008. Despite the economic stasis in Cuba, most younger Cubans have been to university and the literacy race is 99.8 per cent. The government of Cuba is also rightly proud of its incredible health and education systems.

POULTRY

Cuban Roast Chicken with Sour Orange Mojo

Serves 2–4

There is a very popular restaurant in Havana called El Aljibe, which is renowned for its roast chicken and Sour Orange Mojo (the recipe for which is a guarded family secret). The restaurant is named after the chicken farm that was its original supplier. This recipe is inspired by a great evening spent there recently.

4 tablespoons garlic purée
1 teaspoon picked fresh thyme
1 teaspoon dried chilli flakes
100 g fresh white breadcrumbs
1 x 1.5 kg chicken
1 lime, cut in half
olive oil
salt and freshly ground black pepper
a small bunch of fresh thyme,
   to garnish
8 tablespoons Sour Orange Mojo
   (page 119)

Preheat the oven to 190°C/Gas Mark 5.

Put the garlic purée, thyme, chilli flakes and breadcrumbs in a food processor and blitz together. Rub this mixture under the skin of the chicken and place the lime halves inside the cavity.

Brush the chicken with olive oil and season inside and out with salt and pepper. Then truss the bird, as this will hold the stuffing in position; place the chicken on a cutting board with the breast side up. The tail should be facing you. Slip a string under the centre of the chicken's back, making sure that the ends are even. Draw the string up on the sides of the chicken, gently encircling the wings. Tie the ends securely. Roast the chicken in the oven for 1–1¼ hours, or until the bird is golden brown.

While the chicken is roasting, make the Sour Orange Mojo (page 119) and keep warm.

Remove the chicken from the oven and let it rest for 10 minutes. Garnish with a bunch of fresh thyme and some of the Sour Orange Mojo poured over, with the rest served separately in a bowl.

Cubans have a lot to teach us
about taking pleasure in life,
despite the odds. If all we
needed was a bottle of rum
and a boom box to keep us
happy, the world would be a
better place

Chargrilled Chicken Breast with Courgettes, Sultanas and Pine Nuts on a Tomato Mojo

Serve 6

6 small courgettes
5 tablespoons olive oil
2 onions, finely chopped
6 tablespoons sultanas, soaked in
    water for 15 minutes
4 tablespoons toasted pine nuts
6 free range chicken supremes
    (chicken breasts with the small
    bone still attached)
sea salt and freshly ground black
pepper

For the tomato mojo
250 g tomatoes, skinned, de-seeded
    and finely chopped
2 shallots, finely diced
4 tablespoons finely chopped
    fresh parsley
4 tablespoons extra virgin olive oil
2 tablespoons lime juice
salt and freshly ground black pepper

Cut the courgettes into large 5 cm batons. Sprinkle over some sea salt and set aside for 20 minutes. Meanwhile, heat 2 tablespoons of the olive oil in a non-stick saucepan, add the onions, and cook over a slow heat for 10–12 minutes, or until golden and caramelized.

Rinse and dry the courgette batons on absorbent paper, then heat 2 tablespoons of olive oil in a separate frying pan and sauté over a moderate heat for 4–5 minutes, until they are tender and have a little colour.

Add the courgette batons, sultanas and pine nuts to the caramelized onions. Season with pepper only. Keep warm while cooking the chicken.

Heat a griddle pan to high, brush with the remaining oil, then lower the heat and grill the chicken supremes for 6 minutes on each side over a moderate heat. While the chicken is cooking, make the tomato mojo. Place the tomatoes, shallots, parsley, olive oil and lime juice in a saucepan and warm through. Season with salt and pepper.

To assemble, divide the tomato mojo between six warmed plates and spoon over the courgette mixture. Cut each chicken supreme into 2–3 slices lengthwise and fan out on top. Drizzle over any remaining juice.

Spiced Spatchcock of Poussin, Cuban Fufu and Sweetcorn and Black Bean Relish

Serves 4

In Africa, fufu is made from pounded plantains. This version is made with sweet plantains and is flavoured with onions, garlic and smokey bacon. It makes a delicious accompaniment to the poussin and can also be used as a stuffing.

4 x 300 g poussin
2 tablespoons extra virgin olive oil, plus extra to drizzle when serving
2 limes, halved, to garnish
fresh coriander leaves, to garnish

For the spice mix
½ teaspoon sweet paprika
½ teaspoon five spice powder
½ teaspoon ground coriander
½ teaspoon ground cinnamon
½ teaspoon freshly ground black pepper
½ teaspoon Maldon sea salt
½ teaspoon chilli powder
½ teaspoon freshly grated ginger

For the fufu
4 sweet, preferably over-ripe plantains, peeled and roughly chopped
2 tablespoons extra virgin olive oil
100 g streaky smoked bacon, cut into small strips
1 medium onion, diced
3 garlic cloves, crushed

For the sweetcorn and black bean relish
1 tablespoon extra virgin olive oil
1 fresh sweetcorn cob
1 medium red onion, finely diced
400 g tin black beans
1 garlic clove, crushed
2 plum tomatoes, peeled, de-seeded and finely diced
2 tablespoons white wine vinegar
1 tablespoon chopped fresh coriander leaves
salt and freshly ground black pepper
½ red pepper, de-seeded and diced
1 teaspoon Scotch Bonnet hot pepper, de-seeded and finely chopped

To spatchcock the poussin, place each bird breast-side down and, using a very sharp knife, remove the backbone by cutting along either side from neck to bottom. Then flatten the bird with the back of your hand. Turn the legs so that they are facing inwards and cut two incisions, one on each side of the flaps of thigh skin. Thread the legs through and tuck the wings underneath the bird.

For the spice mix, mix all the ingredients together, then spoon into the poussin. Preheat the oven to 180°C/Gas Mark 4.

Heat a griddle pan on the hob, drizzle on ½ tablespoon of olive oil, then add one poussin, breast-side down for 5 minutes. Turn it over and griddle for a further 5 minutes, or until golden-brown on both sides. Repeat the process with the other three poussin.

Transfer the poussin to the oven and roast, breast-side up for 15–20 minutes, or until cooked through and the juices run clear when a thigh is pierced with a skewer.

To make the fufu, place the plantain in a saucepan, cover with lightly salted cold water, bring to the boil and cook for 8–10 minutes, until soft. Drain the water, add 2 tablespoons of olive oil and mash or blitz with a hand-held blender.

Sauté the bacon in a non-stick frying pan for 5 minutes until golden brown. Add the onion and garlic and cook for a further 5 minutes. Remove the excess bacon fat and fold in the mashed plantain. Put to one side, keeping warm.

To make the sweetcorn and black bean relish, rub 1 tablespoon of olive oil over the sweetcorn cob and grill for 10–12 minutes, until very lightly browned all over. Remove the kernels from the cob with a knife and place in a bowl. Toss with all the other relish ingredients, and season well.

To serve, place some of the fufu on a serving dish, add a drizzle of olive oil, layer on the poussin and spoon over some of the relish. Garnish with some fresh coriander leaves and half a lime.

Pan-Fried Spiced Duck Breast with a Piquant Guava Glaze
Serves 4

Guava paste is a rich solid preserve sold in blocks in the markets in Cuba and other Latin countries and is often eaten with fresh cheese. In Cuba, this combination is called Romeo y Juliet.

4 x 175–220 g duck breasts
extra virgin olive oil, for cooking

For the spice mix
½ teaspoon paprika
½ teaspoon ground cumin
½ teaspoon ground coriander
½ teaspoon ground cinnamon
½ teaspoon freshly ground black pepper
½ teaspoon Maldon sea salt
½ teaspoon ground chilli powder
½ teaspoon ground ginger

For the glaze
50 g chopped onion
2 garlic cloves, crushed
6 tablespoons juice from Seville or Sour oranges
juice of 1 lime
1½ tablespoons soy sauce
3½ tablespoons water
1½ tablespoons white wine vinegar
160 g guava jelly or paste (or you could use Spanish quince jelly)
2 teaspoons chopped and de-seeded jalapeño chilli pepper

Hay Que Inventar – you have to be creative – is a Cuban saying. Necessity has been the mother of Cuban creativity, and you find it in small ingenuities – inventing new dishes when ingredients and herbs and spices are sorely lacking

Thoroughly mix all the spices together and put to one side.

For the glaze, place all the glaze ingredients in a pan, bring to the boil and then simmer, stirring all the time, until the guava paste has melted. Remove from the heat, cover with clingfilm, and allow the flavours to infuse for 20 minutes. Pass through a fine sieve and reserve in the fridge.

Trim any excess fat from the duck breasts and lightly score the fat that remains. Rub the spice mixture over the breast and into the scored fat. Leave to marinate for 5 minutes.

Heat a frying pan to a medium to high heat (but not so the olive oil smokes when added), add a drizzle of olive oil, place the duck breasts skin-side down, and cook for about 4 minutes, or until the fat becomes golden brown and crisp. Turn over and cook for a further 3 minutes, until the flesh is pink.

Heat the grill to high. Remove the duck breast from the frying pan and allow to rest in a warm place for 4 minutes. Brush over a generous amount of the glaze and flash under the grill for 1 minute, then rest for 2–3 minutes.

To serve, brush some more of the guava glaze over the breast, then cut into 1.5 cm thick slices. Serve with a crisp green salad.

Guinea Fowl Fricassée

Serves 4

1.6 kg guinea fowl, cut into 12 pieces
1 tablespoon extra virgin olive oil
1 tablespoon brown sugar
2 onions, finely chopped
4 spring onions, finely chopped
3 tomatoes, skinned and chopped
450 ml chicken stock
1 Scotch Bonnet hot pepper (optional)
1 bay leaf
2 tablespoons finely chopped fresh
   parsley, to garnish

For the marinade
juice of 1 lime
2 garlic cloves, chopped
1 teaspoon dried oregano
½ teaspoon ground cumin
salt and freshly ground black pepper

Mix all the marinade ingredients together
in a small bowl and put to one side.

Put the pieces of guinea fowl in a large
bowl and pour over the marinade. Marinate
for 2 hours, turning occasionally. Drain and
reserve the marinade.

In a large saucepan or ovenproof casserole
dish, carefully heat the olive oil and sugar
together over a moderate heat until the
sugar begins to caramelize. Add half the
pieces of guinea fowl at a time and brown
for 15 minutes, turning frequently. Remove
with a slotted spoon.

Place the onions and spring onions in the
same pan and fry for 5 minutes, adding a
little more oil if necessary. Stir frequently.

Stir in the tomatoes and cook for 5 minutes.
Pour over the stock and the reserved
marinade, then add the Scotch Bonnet hot
pepper (if using) and bay leaf, and bring to
the boil. Return the guinea fowl to the pan
and lower the heat. Simmer for 20–30
minutes, or until the guinea fowl is tender.
Taste and adjust the seasoning.

Before serving, remove the Scotch Bonnet
hot pepper (if using) and bay leaf and
garnish with the parsley.

When the Soviet Union crumbled in 1989, a new low-input sustainable agriculture that was not dependent on imports was required. A savvy Castro recognised this. He stated in 1991, 'Our problems must be solved without feed-stocks, fertilisers or fuel.' Although this enterprise was originally a reactionary policy designed to combat economic isolation, today the organic mentality has taken hold and Cuba, despite its continuing challenges, is one of the healthiest countries to live in

MEAT

Roast Rack of Lamb with Giant Butter Beans, Tomatoes and Coriander

Serves 4

250 g dried giant butter beans, covered
   with water and soaked overnight
½ onion
1 carrot
1 celery stick
1 bay leaf
375 ml Chunky Tomato Sauce (page 118)
4 x 4-bone rack lamb
1 tablespoon extra virgin olive oil
425 g plum tomatoes, skinned,
   de-seeded and diced
2 tablespoons finely chopped
   fresh coriander
salt and freshly ground black pepper

Drain the soaked butter beans, put them in
a large saucepan and add the onion, carrot,
celery stick and bay leaf. Cover with water
and cook over a moderate heat for
45 minutes to 1 hour, or until tender. Drain.

Preheat the oven to 200°C/Gas Mark 6. Warm
the chunky tomato sauce in a saucepan,
then add the beans. Season well and set
aside. Season the lamb racks and roast in
the oven for 25 minutes. Remove from the
oven and set aside to rest for 5–10 minutes.

Meanwhile, heat the olive oil in a saucepan,
add the plum tomatoes, cook for 5 minutes
and then add the butter beans. Stir in the
coriander and season to taste. Cut each
rack into cutlets and cover with the giant
butter beans.

Picanha Steak with Farofa

Serves 4

Farofa (also called gari) is grated cassava,
dried and toasted. Cassava (called yuca in
Cuba) is a starch and flour produce used
widely in South America and all over the
Caribbean. Asking a Cuban friend of mine
how he regarded himself – as Caribbean or
Latin American – he answered both. So on
that basis I have expanded my ingredients to
include some Latin American produce. Farofa
is available in African, Portuguese and South
American stores as well as some large
supermarkets.

1 kg beef topside rump
100 g streaky bacon, diced
15 g butter
1 small onion, chopped
125 g farofa
freshly ground black pepper
8 tablespoons Chimmichurri Dressing
   (page 122)
2 tablespoons finely chopped
   fresh parsley

Cut the beef lengthwise into 250 g steak
portions, then season with pepper.

Over a low heat, fry the bacon in a dry pan
for several minutes until it begins to
colour. Add the butter and onion, cook for
3 minutes, then add the farofa and cook
1–2 minutes.

Heat the grill to high, then cook the beef
steaks for 1–2 minutes on each side for
rare, 2–3 minutes for medium rare, 4–5

minutes for medium and 5–6 minutes for
well done. (These times, of course, will
depend on how thick the steaks are.) Set
aside and rest for five minutes before
serving.

To serve, place some farofa in the centre of
a plate. Slice the beef steaks and fan over
the top. Drizzle over plenty of the
Chimmichurri Dressing and sprinkle on
the parsley.

Roast Suckling Pig

Serves 6–8

Suckling pig is one of the classic Cuban dishes served at a special event. It is often cooked on a spit over an open fire but tastes just as good cooked in a conventional oven.

2.75 kg suckling piglet
200 g coarse sea salt
160 ml extra virgin olive oil
150 g butter
2 carrots, sliced into four pieces each
1 onion, coarsely chopped
zest and juice of 1 sour orange
salt and freshly ground black pepper

Heat the oven to 220°C/Gas Mark 7.

Wash and dry the piglet. Then rub it all over with the coarse sea salt and set aside for 30 minutes. Wash the salt off and pat the meat dry. Season with a little salt and pepper, inside and out. Wrap the ears with aluminium foil to prevent them from burning.

Place the piglet in a large roasting pan. Baste with olive oil and dot all over with the butter.

Place in the oven and roast, basting often with the pan drippings for about 2½ hours.

About 10 minutes before removing the piglet from the oven, add the carrots, onion, orange zest and juice to the pan. Remove the piglet from the oven when it is fully cooked, checking first that the meat

juices run clear without any sign of blood. Remove the aluminium foil from the ears and place the piglet on a serving dish. Keep warm while you make the gravy.

Pour the juices from the roasting pan into a saucepan with the vegetables and place over a medium heat on the hob. When the juices start to sizzle, skim the fat off the top. Add 500 ml of water to the pan. Increase the heat to high and boil rapidly for 5 minutes to reduce the juices. Strain through a metal strainer or cheesecloth.

Serve the piglet on a large platter with the warm gravy on the side.

Meatballs Stuffed with Quails' Eggs in Tomato Sauce

Serves 6

18 quails' eggs, hard-boiled (for
 approximately 5 minutes)
4 tablespoons olive oil
125 g fresh spinach

For the meatballs
2 garlic cloves, crushed
1 onion, chopped
100 g minced beef
225 g minced pork
1 free range organic egg,
 lightly beaten
2 slices of white bread, crusts removed
 and soaked in milk
1 teaspoon ground cumin
a generous pinch of ground cloves
1 tablespoon chopped fresh oregano
½ teaspoon salt
a small pinch of freshly ground
 black pepper

For the oregano and tomato sauce
2 tablespoons olive oil
1 medium onion, finely chopped
2 garlic cloves, finely chopped
450 g fresh plum tomatoes, skinned,
 de-seeded and chopped
150 g tinned plum tomatoes
1 teaspoon salt
freshly ground black pepper
1 teaspoon sugar
2 teaspoons chopped fresh oregano
 (or ½ teaspoon dried oregano)

First make the meatballs. Blitz all the ingredients in a food processor. Take a handful of the mixture and flatten it out in your hand. Place a cooked quail's egg in the centre and press the mixture around it to form a meatball. Repeat this procedure with the remaining quails' eggs and set aside.

Next, make the tomato sauce. Heat 2 tablespoons of oil in a saucepan, add the onion and fry for 5–8 minutes until soft. Stir in the garlic and cook for a further 2 minutes. Then add the tomatoes, salt, pepper, sugar and oregano and cook for a further 15 minutes. Remove from the heat, allow to cool slightly, then push the sauce through a sieve into a saucepan using the back of a wooden spoon. Transfer half of the tomato sauce to a bowl and put the other half in a saucepan. Set both aside.

Heat the 4 tablespoons of oil in a frying pan and fry the meatballs over a moderate heat for 15 minutes, turning frequently. Warm the saucepan containing half of the reserved tomato sauce, then add the fried meatballs and cook for a further 15 minutes. Warm up the remaining tomato sauce in a separate saucepan.

To serve, place a handful of the fresh spinach in the centre of each plate. Place three meatballs on top of each pile of spinach and spoon over some of the warmed tomato sauce.

Time and technology have stood still

A drive through the countryside of Cuba offers unforgettable images of life where time and technology have stood still. Images of the red baking earth soaking up tropical rains. Fields criss-crossed with humid tracts of sugar cane or traversed by loping cattle. Clouds that move quickly across the sun, offering respite from the heat of the bright blue sky. Cowboy-hatted farmers in spurs riding horses and carts down dusty orange roads with oxen ploughing the rich soil in the neighbouring farms. Happy families rocking on porches towered over by royal palms and tobacco fields, as their chickens and the family pig potter in the background.

Oxtail with Aged Rum and Rioja Wine

Serves 6

2 oxtails, cut into serving pieces,
   trimmed of excess fat
2 tablespoons olive oil
4 garlic cloves
250 g boniato (sweet potato),
   peeled and cubed
3 onions, sliced
250 g calabaza (pumpkin),
   cubed (available from Afro-Caribbean
   and ethnic grocers)
250 g celeriac, peeled and cubed
300 ml beef stock
600 ml Rioja wine
1 Scotch Bonnet hot pepper (optional)
1 teaspoon allspice berries
2 cinnamon sticks

2 bay leaves
2 tablespoons tomato purée
zest and juice of 1 lime
1 teaspoon sugar
salt and freshly ground black pepper
150 ml aged rum
2 tablespoons finely chopped fresh
   flat leaf parsley, to garnish

For the seasoning
3 garlic cloves
1 red onion, finely chopped
1 teaspoon fresh oregano leaves
2 teaspoons finely chopped, de-seeded
   Scotch Bonnet hot pepper (optional)
1 celery stick, chopped

Blanch the oxtail pieces by pouring boiling
water over them. Dry thoroughly with
kitchen paper and place in a bowl. Blitz all
the seasoning ingredients in a food

processor, then rub the mixture over the meat. Cover and place in the refrigerator to marinate overnight.

Heat the olive oil in a ovenproof casserole or large saucepan, add the oxtail pieces, a few at a time, and fry for 5–7 minutes, or until the meat is lightly browned. As each batch is done, remove with a slotted spoon and set aside in a bowl.

Once all the meat has been browned and set aside, add the garlic, sweet potato, onions, pumpkin and celeriac to the casserole and fry over a moderate heat for 5 minutes, or until golden brown.

Drain off any excess fat (if any), pour in the stock, wine and 300 ml water, then return the meat to the casserole. Add the Scotch Bonnet hot pepper (if using), allspice

berries, cinnamon sticks, bay leaves, tomato purée and lime zest and juice. Season with the sugar, salt and pepper.

Bring to the boil over a moderate heat, then reduce the heat to low and simmer for 2½–3 hours, or until the meat is soft and tender. Remove the Scotch Bonnet hot pepper (if using) and discard. Transfer the meat to a warmed serving dish and keep warm while you finish the sauce.

Strain the sauce juices through a sieve into another pan, pressing out as much liquid as possible from the vegetables with the back of a wooden spoon. De-glaze the casserole with the rum and then add to the strained sauce in the pan. Bring the sauce to the boil, then remove from the heat and pour over the oxtail. Serve immediately, garnished with the chopped parsley.

Pot Roast Belly of Pork, Pig Cheeks and Morcilla Sausage

Serves 6

6 tablespoons extra virgin olive oil, plus
   extra for drizzling
1 kg pork belly, skin scored, rubbed with
   1 tablespoon of salt, left overnight,
   then rinsed off and dried
coarsely ground black pepper
1 tablespoon fennel seeds
root vegetables: 1 onion, halved;
   2 whole celery sticks; 2 carrots;
   1 garlic clove, cut in half
500 g pig cheeks
3 onions, diced
4 garlic cloves, crushed
2 tablespoons flour
1 bay leaf
150 ml red wine
800 ml chicken stock
2 medium red onions, cut lengthways
250 g whole small carrots
3 celery sticks, diced
3 sprigs of fresh thyme
500 g morcilla sausage with
   onion (blood sausage), cut diagonally
   into 1 cm slices
150 g tomatoes, skinned, de-seeded
   and diced
salt and freshly ground black pepper
1 tablespoon fresh flat leaf parsley,
   finely chopped, to garnish

Preheat the oven to 140°C/Gas Mark 1.

Drizzle 2 tablespoons of olive oil over the salted belly of pork and season it with coarsely ground black pepper and fennel seeds. Arrange the root vegetables and garlic on the base of a roasting tin (these act as a trivet to lift the meat away from the direct heat of the base of the tin) and slow-roast the pork for 2 hours, or until the crackling is crisp.

After 1 hour, prepare the pig cheeks. Heat 2 tablespoons of olive oil in an ovenproof casserole or baking dish, add the diced onions and garlic and sweat over a low heat for 10 minutes. Put aside. Flour and season the pig's cheeks. Heat 2 tablespoons of olive oil in a separate non-stick frying pan and pan-fry the cheeks for 6 minutes on each side until golden brown.

Add the pig cheeks to the onion mixture. Add the bay leaf and red wine and pour over the chicken stock. Place in the oven and slowly braise for 1 hour, or until tender. Remove from the oven, set aside and keep warm.

Increase the oven temperature to high. 220°C/Gas Mark 7. Put the red onions, whole small carrots and celery on a baking sheet. Drizzle with olive oil and season. Add the thyme sprigs and roast for 5 minutes.

On a separate baking sheet, roast the morcilla sausage for 5 minutes. Remove from the oven and set aside, keeping warm.

To serve, cut the belly of pork into slices and place on a serving dish. Cut the pig cheeks in half and add them to the dish with the cooking liquid. Finally, add the morcilla sausage and roasted vegetables, garnish with the diced tomato and sprinkle with the chopped parsley.

Beef and Chorizo Fritas (Cuban Burgers)

Serves 4

These beef and chorizo fritas, or Cuban hamburgers, are for serious carnivores. The combination of the beef, pork and chorizo gives a delicious new twist to your regular burgers. The only thing is that you need a big mouth to eat them!

550 g minced beef
150 g minced pork
150 g minced chorizo
1 egg yolk
1 medium onion, finely chopped
1 garlic clove, finely chopped
¼ teaspoon ground cumin
salt

For the garnish
4 x flatbreads or large burger buns
pickled gherkins
1 tomato, diced
⅛ shredded iceberg lettuce
1 red onion, diced
3–4 tablespoons mayonnaise

Mix the beef, pork, chorizo, egg yolk, onion, garlic and cumin together in a large bowl. Season to taste with salt. Form into four large burgers and set aside.

Heat a grill or griddle pan to high and grill the burgers for 4–5 minutes on each side (or more, depending on how you like them).

Serve in a flatbread or burger bun with pickled gherkins, tomato, lettuce, onion and mayonnaise.

'Inside the Revolution: everything. Outside the Revolution: nothing!' FIDEL CASTRO

Cuban literature began to find its voice in the early 19th century, when major works were abolitionist in character. When slavery was abolished in 1886, independence and freedom became the main theme, exemplified by José Marti, Castro's hero, who led the modernista movement in Latin American literature.

At the time of the Revolution, Cuba's biggest writers were Alejo Carpentier and the poet José Lezama Lima. Lima scandalised post-revolutionary Cuba with accounts of his gay experiences in *Paradiso* (1966). In the post-revolutionary era, many writers exiled themselves, but in recent years a Cuban boom has seen writers born during or after the revolutionary movement come to the fore.

Braised Rabbit Cannelloni, Sweet Potato and Chorizo Sausage

Serves 8

Rabbit is a popular meat in Cuba; it has a delicate flavour and has the advantage of being very low in fat. Many of the urban farmers produce excellent rabbit meat.

½ rabbit, skinned, head and guts
    removed, washed, dried and cut in half
3 tablespoons olive oil
150 g cooking chorizo, minced
200 g onions, finely diced
2 garlic cloves, crushed
½ bottle of white wine
1 bay leaf
600 ml chicken stock, or enough
    to cover the rabbit
200 g sweet potato, peeled and diced

2 tablespoons butter
2 shallots, finely diced
200 g baby spinach leaves,
    blanched and drained
1 tablespoon chopped fresh sage
50 g white bread, crusts removed
    and soaked in 2 tablespoons of milk
2 tablespoons chopped fresh parsley
1 egg yolk
½ teaspoon ground nutmeg
2 tablespoons finely grated
    Parmesan cheese
350 g fresh lasagne sheets,
    cut into 16 pieces
300 ml Chunky Tomato Sauce (page 118)
salt and freshly ground black pepper

For the topping
500 ml Béchamel Sauce (page 122)
2 tablespoons freshly grated
    Parmesan cheese

For the garnish
fresh cilantro or coriander
fresh basil
fresh Italian parsley

Preheat the oven to 180°C/Gas Mark 4.

Season the rabbit pieces. Heat the olive oil in a large frying pan and fry the rabbit until golden brown on all sides. Remove and place the rabbit in a heavy roasting tray. Put the minced chorizo in the frying pan and gently fry for 5 minutes. Add the onions and garlic and cook for 5–7 minutes, or until lightly coloured. Place in the roasting tray with the rabbit.

De-glaze the hot frying pan with the white wine and pour the wine over the rabbit. Add the bay leaf and pour in enough chicken stock to cover the rabbit.

Bring the chicken stock to the boil, skim away any fat that comes to the top, cover with a lid and put the roasting tray in the oven for about 1 hour, until the rabbit meat is falling off the bone. Take the rabbit out of the cooking juices and allow to cool.

Pour the juices from the roasting pan into a blender and liquidize, then pass the juices through a fine sieve into a saucepan. Place the pan over a high heat, bring it to the boil and cook for 30–40 minutes, or until the juices have reduced to a glaze or sticky consistency. Put to one side.

Sauté the sweet potato in 1 tablespoon of butter for 5 minutes. It should start to cook but still be al dente. Remove from the heat.

Once the rabbit has cooled, pull all the meat from the bone and loosely shred. Place in a large mixing bowl.

Sweat the shallots in the remainder of the butter until soft, then stir in the spinach and sage. Add this to the shredded rabbit meat, then add the soaked bread, parsley, egg yolk, nutmeg, sweet potato, Parmesan cheese and half the reduced stock.

Mix well, trying not to break the meat down further. Season to taste (you may not need salt because the stock will have enough). If the mixture looks a bit dry, add some more of the reduced stock.

Lay out the pieces of pasta on a floured worktop. Spoon on the rabbit mixture between all 16 pieces of pasta, and roll each into a cannelloni tube. Chill for 15 minutes.

Preheat the oven to 180°C/Gas Mark 4.

Spread the Chunky Tomato Sauce over the bottom of a large baking dish. Place the cannelloni on top of the tomato sauce in neat rows. Cover with the Béchamel Sauce and scatter the Parmesan cheese over the top. Cover with foil.

Bake for 20 minutes and then remove the foil and bake for a further 10–15 minutes, until golden brown and bubbling. Remove and leave to stand for 10 minutes.

Roughly tear the fresh herbs, scatter over the top and serve.

Roast Leg of Organic Kid and Mint Salsa with Roast Vegetables

Serves 4

If you are unable to find organic kid or goat meat, use organic spring lamb instead.

1 tablespoon cumin seeds
4 garlic cloves, peeled
olive oil
1 red chilli, de-seeded and sliced
1 teaspoon picked fresh thyme
1 x 1–1.5 kg leg of organic spring kid
salt and freshly ground black pepper

For the spicy roast vegetables

2 large red onions, cut in half
1 large sweet potato, cut into
   2.5 cm chunks
1 garlic bulb, cut horizontally in half
400 g small new potatoes, washed
1 green plantain, peeled and sliced
   into 2.5 cm discs
1 red chilli, de-seeded and sliced in half
1 green chilli
olive oil
salt and freshly ground black pepper

For the mint salsa

2 tablespoons chopped fresh mint
½ teaspoon chopped fresh coriander
2 shallots, finely diced
2 teaspoons freshly grated root ginger
zest and juice of 1 lime
1 large tomato, skinned and
   de-seeded, finely diced
4 tablespoons extra virgin olive oil
salt and freshly ground black pepper

If you can, make the seasoning the day before. Preheat the oven to 140°C/Gas Mark 1. Sprinkle the cumin seeds on to a baking sheet and place in the oven to toast for 5 minutes, or until light brown. Toss the garlic cloves in a little olive oil and season with some salt. Place in the oven for 15–20 minutes, until softened but not mushy. In a pestle and mortar, grind the roasted cumin seeds with the red chilli, roasted garlic and thyme. Make some gashes in the meat with a sharp knife. Rub the spice mixture into the meat and each incision. Cover and refrigerate overnight.

Remove the meat from the fridge a good hour before you want to cook it. Preheat the oven to 200°C/Gas Mark 6 and season the meat well.

Put a large roasting pan (to fit the vegetables and the meat) in the oven for 5 minutes to get hot. Remove the pan, drizzle in some olive oil, add the meat and roast for 15 minutes. Turn and roast for a further 15 minutes. Remove the pan, scatter all the ingredients for the spicy roast vegetables around the meat and turn them once to coat with the juices. Roast for further 45 minutes–1 hour. The meat should be medium to medium-well done, depending on your preference.

While the meat is cooking, make the mint salsa. Mix all the ingredients together and set aside.

Remove the meat from the oven and leave it to rest in a warm place for 15 minutes. Turn the vegetables once more and then place them on a warmed serving dish. Carve the kid and cover with some of the salsa. Serve with the spicy roasted vegetables and some white rice or a puréed starch.

Cuban Fried Pork

Serves 4

Along with chicken, pork is the favourite meat of most Cubans. It is sold at street stalls in Havana and in markets throughout Cuba. The flesh is white and clean and most of the pigs are raised organically. I have to say that it is some of the best pork I have ever tasted.

1 kg boneless lean pork (leg or shoulder) cut into 5 cm cubes, washed and dried
salt and freshly ground black pepper
4 garlic cloves, crushed
125 ml sour orange juice from Seville oranges; or a mix of orange and lemon juice
2 tablespoons lime juice
approx 150 ml vegetable oil
Mojo Criollo (page 116)

Season the meat well with salt and pepper, then thoroughly rub the garlic into the meat. Place the meat in a large glass or plastic bowl, pour over the orange and lime juices, cover and refrigerate overnight or for a minimum of 3 hours.

Drain the pork and pat dry. Heat the oil in a saucepan until very hot but not smoking. Add the pork in small batches (don't overcrowd) and fry for 6–8 minutes, turning with a spoon, until golden brown on the outside and soft and cooked through in the middle. (Cook for a little longer if you like your meat well done.)

Remove the pork, pat out any excess oil, and keep warm until all the pork is cooked. Place in a serving dish and serve with lots of Mojo Criollo over the top. This dish would traditionally be served with Moros y Cristianos (page 108), Tostones (page 103) and a mixed salad.

Baseball was introduced to Cuba in the 1860s by Cubans who studied in the United States and American sailors who ported in the country. The sport quickly spread across the island when preferences switched to baseball from watching bullfights, which Cubans were expected to attend as homage to their Spanish rulers. Consequently, baseball became a symbol of freedom and egalitarianism for the Cuban people.

Baseball is the Cuban national sport

'The most futile and disastrous day seems well spent when it is reviewed through the blue, fragrant smoke of a Havana Cigar'

EVELYN WAUGH

Cuba is famous worldwide for its fine cigars: amongst the many brands, Monte Christo – favoured by Che Guevara – Romeo and Juliet and Patagas; Cohiba is regarded as the best cigar. With an intense and aromatic flavour, it is made from the best quality leaves, from the best region, picked in the best season. And rolled by the best cigar rollers.

The major tobacco growing areas, Vuelta Abajo (Pinar del Rio Province) and Vuelta Arriba (Villa Clara Province) have the choicest small plots, producing the finest leaves. Since 1959, all 60 plantations, factories, brands and profits have been state-controlled.

A visit to the Patagas cigar factory in Havana is enlightening. There you can learn everything there is to know about the ubiquitous Cuban cigar and why it deserves its reputation as being the finest there is.

Cigar-making is a very complex process. The task of sorting the leaves, the rolling and packing is all done by hand. They don't work in teams – one person does everything and each worker has a quota of 110 cigars a day. It is a prized job in Cuba and workers have to train for 9 months and take exams in the attached cigar school, after which they are looked after very well. There is a stage at the front of the factory where a reader sits with a microphone and will read out a story and the news to the workers. This is repeated again in the afternoon. They also listen to a soap opera on the radio each day. This happens every day at the same time in every cigar factory in Cuba.

The cigars are also sorted by colours – they have eight colours and 17 shades – before they are put in the box. This is purely cosmetic because colour never affects taste.

It takes five different types of leaves to make a cigar. The best-looking leaf is kept for the wrapper. Inside, four leaves create the taste; the combustion, the aroma, the strength and the binder. The leaves are sorted in different sizes and textures, then stretched, sprayed with water and dried. After the roller has mixed the leaves, the rolled leaves are placed in a mould and, once full, the mould goes inside a press for 30 minutes. Each wrapper is then stuck on with natural glue from the sap of a maple tree. The Draw Master machine then checks the pressure for the draw – to tell if the leaves have been rolled too tight or too loosely. Finally, each cedar wood cigar box has the government stamp, the habanos stamp and a holographic stamp.

VEGETARIAN

Tempura of Vegetables Japino Latino Style
Serves 6

One of the most expensive and interesting restaurants in Havana is housed in an elegant old Miramar mansion. Named after Cuba's national bird, Tocororo, it has the distinction of having no fixed menu. The waiter tells you what is on the menu that day and you can choose how you wish it to be cooked. It also has a little sushi bar and restaurant, Sakura, which serves traditional Japanese food.

When cooking tempura, ensure you use a fresh selection of vegetables. The following may be substituted by a variety of your own choice.

800 ml vegetable oil, for frying
1 carrot, cut into thin sticks
½ onion, sliced
1 green pepper, cut into rings
    and de-seeded
1 aubergine, thinly sliced
6 broccoli florets, blanched for a
    couple of minutes
1 medium courgette
6 button mushrooms
6 asparagus spears, trimmed
18 mangetout
½ butternut squash, peeled
    and cut into 12 bite-size pieces

For the batter
2 free range organic eggs
300 ml iced water
360 g plain flour, sieved

For the dip
4 tablespoons mirin (a Japanese rice
    wine condiment, similar to sake)
4 tablespoons sake
100 ml light soy sauce
1–2 tablespoons freshly grated ginger

First make the batter. Using a fork, roughly mix together the eggs, iced water and flour (tempura batter should be a bit lumpy.) Set aside.

Then make the dip. Mix together all the ingredients and pour into a serving bowl.

Heat the vegetable oil over a moderate heat in a deep-sided frying pan until the oil is hot enough to deep fry. You can test this by dropping in a cube of bread – it should turn golden brown in a few moments.

Dip the vegetables in the batter a few at a time and fry them in batches, keeping each batch warm while you fry the rest.

Serve hot with the dipping sauce.

Mozzarella, Aubergine, Spinach and Basil Quesadilla
Makes 4

1 aubergine
5 free range organic eggs, beaten
50 g freshly grated Parmesan cheese
4 tablespoons plain flour, plus extra
    for dusting
8 tablespoons olive oil
2 shallots, chopped

1 garlic clove, crushed
200 g spinach, blanched in
   boiling water for a few seconds,
   water squeezed out
8 flour tortillas (approx 15 cm
   diameter)
4 jalapeño chilli peppers (optional),
   de-seeded and finely chopped
200 g Buffalo mozzarella, thinly sliced
12 large fresh basil leaves
salt and freshly ground pepper

Slice and salt the aubergine, leave for
½ hour, rinse and pat dry.

Beat four of the eggs with the Parmesan
cheese. Sprinkle the flour over the
aubergine slices, dip them in the egg mix
and shallow-fry in 4 tablespoons of the
olive oil over a low heat. Leave to cool.

Preheat the oven to 180°C/Gas Mark 4.

Sweat the shallots and garlic in 1
tablespoon of olive oil until soft. Add the
spinach and season well. Leave to cool.

Dust the work surface with flour and lay
out four flour tortillas. Cover the tortillas
with the spinach mixture (leaving the
edges clear) and sprinkle on the jalapeño
chilli peppers. Add the mozzarella slices,
followed by the basil leaves and the slices
of aubergine.

Brush the remaining beaten egg over the
edges of the tortillas and lay another
tortilla on top. Press together to form a
sandwich effect.

Brush the tortilla sandwiches with the
remaining oil and pan fry in an ovenproof
pan with a metal handle for 3–4 minutes,
or until they are golden brown. Then place
the pan in the oven for 5 minutes until the
tops are brown. Serve immediately.

Roasted Vegetable Tart

Serves 8

150 g plain flour, plus a little extra
   for rolling out
a pinch of salt
60 g butter, cubed, plus 1 tablespoon
   to grease the baking tray
4 red onions, sliced
4 garlic cloves
6 sprigs of thyme
1 x 400 g tin palm hearts, drained
1 red pepper, de-seeded, and cut
   into chunky strips
1 orange pepper, de-seeded and
   cut into chunky strips
1 yellow pepper, de-seeded and
   cut into chunky strips

3 tablespoons stoned and halved
   black olives
2 tablespoons capers
3 tablespoons extra virgin olive oil
salt and freshly ground black pepper

For the accompanying salsa
4 large vine tomatoes, finely chopped
½ red onion, finely chopped
a large handful of basil leaves, finely
   chopped
2 teaspoons Tabasco

Put the flour and salt in a large bowl and
add the cubes of butter. Use your fingertips
to rub the butter into the flour until the
mixture resembles coarse breadcrumbs.
Try to work quickly so that it does not
become greasy.

Using a knife, stir in 2–3 tablespoons of cold water, or just enough for a dough to bind together. Wrap the dough in clingfilm and refrigerate for 10–15 minutes before using.

Preheat the oven to 200°C/Gas Mark 6.

In a pan, gently sweat the red onions and garlic in 1 tablespoon of olive oil over a low heat for 5–8 minutes, until soft and beginning to caramelize. Season with salt, pepper and half a tablespoon of thyme, picked from the sprigs.

Place the palm hearts and the red, orange and yellow peppers in a roasting tin. Add the remaining oil and four of the thyme sprigs. Season with salt and pepper and mix well. Roast in the oven for 20 minutes, remove and then set aside.

Grease a 22 cm pastry tin with the tablespoon of butter. Flour a cool surface and roll out the dough to line the tin to a thickness of about 5 mm. Bake blind in the oven for 15 minutes or until golden brown.

Remove the pastry from the oven and fill with an even layer of the onions and garlic, then cover with the roasted peppers and palm hearts, olives and capers. Sprinkle over the remaining thyme, picked from the sprigs, and return to the oven for 5–10 minutes.

For the accompanying salsa, mix together the tomatoes, onion and basil. Add the Tabasco, season well and mix again. Serve the vegetable tart in slices, with the salsa on the side.

Aubergine and Okra Gratin in a Béchamel Sauce

Serves 4

180 g okra, washed and sliced
sea salt
4 medium aubergines,
   topped and tailed, flesh hollowed
   out and roughly chopped, aubergine
   shells reserved
2 tablespoons extra virgin olive oil
60 g butter
200 g courgettes, diced
300 g onions, sliced
60 g unsalted cashew nuts
2 tablespoons chopped fresh
   flat leaf parsley
150 g tinned plum tomatoes, drained
200 g Chunky Tomato Sauce (page 118)
150 g Béchamel Sauce (page 122)
40 g freshly grated Parmesan cheese
salt and freshly ground black pepper

Preheat the oven to 180°C/Gas Mark 4.

First, blanch the okra. Rub the okra with sea salt, then set aside for 10 minutes. Rinse off the salt and blanch the okra in boiling water for 2 minutes, then set aside.

Season the aubergine shells with salt and pepper. Brush with the olive oil and place on a roasting tray. Place in the oven for 15–20 minutes, or until they appear soft but are still holding their form.

Warm the butter in a saucepan over a moderate heat, add the diced aubergine and cook for 5 minutes. Add the courgettes and onions and cook for a further 8 minutes. Reduce the heat to low, stir in the cashew nuts, parsley and plum tomatoes and cook for a further 10 minutes.

Meanwhile, gently cook the okra and the Chunky Tomato Sauce in a pan for 6 minutes.

Remove the aubergine shells from the oven and fill them with the vegetable mix. Spoon the Béchamel Sauce over the vegetables, then return the aubergines to the oven and cook for a further 15 minutes.

Preheat the grill to high. Remove the aubergines from the oven, sprinkle over the Parmesan cheese and place them under the preheated grill for 3 minutes.

To serve, put a mound of okra in the centre of the plate and place the aubergines on top.

MUSIC AND

Wherever you go in Cuba, you will find a soundtrack – whether from a pair of tinny speakers or a street-corner rumba. You'd have to be a real party pooper not to be moved by this. The most distinctive part of Cuban culture is its rich heritage of music and dancing. Salsa, son and rumba trace their roots to Cuba.

Cuba's music origins are a fusion of Hispanic and West African music, brought by slaves who tapped out rhythms on barrels. Lately, modern music from the US and elsewhere has added to the mix. Reggaeton, for example, blends the Jamaican music influences of reggae and dancehall with those of Latin America, giving Cuban youth a musical genre that they can relate to.

However, the classic dance styles are still prevalent, with a resurgence in Cuban dances such as the salsa, son, rumba, mambo and cha-cha-cha. Most of these routines are derived from son, a distinctly Afro-Cuban musical style combining Spanish poetic lyrics and plucked instruments.

Mambo means 'conversation with the gods' and is sometimes referred to as the 'diabolo', the devil's dance.

DANCING

An intrinsic style of Cuban cançion, or song, is musica guajira ('cowboy music') from the rural areas of western and central Cuba, with its Spanish influences. Guitar and string instruments accompany these songs, which echo North American country music and blues songs. In 1996 a group of talented older Cuban musicians, The Buena Vista Social Club, was 'rediscovered' by Ry Cooder, raising international awareness of the many styles of classic Cuban folk music and salsa.

ON THE SIDE

Roasted Pumpkin with Mint and Honey Dressing

Serves 4

800 g pumpkin or butternut squash, peeled and cut into wedges
½ teaspoon dried red chilli flakes
6 sprigs of fresh thyme
3 tablespoons extra virgin olive oil
sea salt

For the dressing
75 ml clear honey
75 ml red wine vinegar
a large handful of fresh mint leaves

Preheat the oven to 200°C/Gas Mark 6.

Place the pumpkin or squash on a roasting tray, scatter over the chilli flakes and thyme sprigs, toss well with the olive oil, and season with the salt. Roast in the preheated oven for 35–40 minutes, until golden.

Meanwhile, make the dressing: place the honey and vinegar in a saucepan, bring to the boil, then simmer for 5 minutes.

Place the roasted pumpkin on a serving dish, pour on the dressing and scatter over the mint leaves.

Spiced Beetroot

Serves 6–8

4 large beetroots, weighing about 750 g in total
1 large Spanish onion, sliced
2 tablespoons caster sugar
1 tablespoon finely chopped fresh ginger
150 ml cane vinegar or distilled white malt vinegar
60 ml water
1 tablespoon allspice berries (optional)
2 whole cloves
½ Scotch Bonnet hot pepper, de-seeded and sliced

Boil the beetroots in a large saucepan of water for 45–60 minutes, or until tender. Set aside to cool slightly, then remove the skin and cut into slices. Place in a shallow bowl with the sliced onion.

Heat the sugar, ginger, vinegar, water, allspice berries (if using), cloves and Scotch Bonnet hot pepper in a saucepan until just boiling. Remove from the heat and pour over the beetroot and onions. Set aside to cool.

Serve when cold (the longer this sits, the better it tastes). It will also keep for several weeks in the fridge.

LA LUCHA

Cubans, used to putting up with the everyday struggles of life, or 'la lucha' (the struggle), use their own brand of black humour (as well as music, dancing, rum and Santeria) to off-set living on rations, the horrors of public transport, the likelihood of one's house falling down any day and the fact that there is nowhere to go if you want to escape the in-laws or the parents (there is a general housing shortage), except the street.

Black Bean Stew

Serves 10

325 g dried black beans
3 tablespoons extra virgin olive oil
1 medium onion, finely chopped
6 garlic cloves, finely chopped
2 green peppers, finely chopped
1 teaspoon picked fresh oregano leaves
1 teaspoon ground cumin
1 bay leaf
2 tablespoons red wine vinegar
6 tablespoons white wine
1 teaspoon sugar
salt and freshly ground black pepper

For the garnish
1 onion, finely chopped
1 tablespoon picked fresh
   oregano leaves
a drizzle of extra virgin olive oil

Wash the beans, then transfer them to a bowl, cover with plenty of cold water and soak overnight.

The next day, rinse the beans again and transfer to a saucepan. Pour in 1 litre of water and 1 tablespoon of the olive oil. Bring to the boil over a high heat, reduce the heat to low and simmer for 1 hour. Don't add salt. Set aside but don't drain.

In another saucepan, heat 2 tablespoons of the olive oil, add the onion, garlic, green peppers and oregano leaves and sweat over a low heat for 5 minutes.

Stir in the ground cumin and bay leaf, and cook for 1 more minute. Spoon in the beans with their juices, add the vinegar and wine, then simmer over a low heat for 15 minutes. Remove and discard the bay leaf.

Transfer ¼ of the beans to a bowl and mash lightly with a fork. Return the mixture to the pan. Add the sugar and season with salt and freshly ground black pepper.

Serve in a bowl garnished with the chopped onion, fresh oregano leaves and a drizzle of olive oil.

Tostone Fritters with Cuban Aïoli

Serves 6

Tostones are fried green plantains and they are a staple in the Cuban diet. They are a starchy, savoury bite and are characterized by the cooking method of double frying. Tostone purists will always use an entirely green and sugar-free plantain to make their tostones.

1 kg very green plantain
400 ml vegetable oil for deep-frying
salt
Cuban Aïoli Sauce (page 122)

Peel the plantain and cut into 5 cm chunks. Heat the oil in a deep fryer or large saucepan until it is moderately hot. Add the plantain chunks and blanch for 5 minutes, or until soft. Using a slotted spoon, remove from the oil and drain on some kitchen paper. Set aside to cool.

When cooled, press the plantain chunks with a flat object to make 2 x 2 cm pieces. Set aside to cool completely then reheat the oil until hot and bubbling and deep-fry the plantain for a few minutes, or until they are crisp. Drain on kitchen towels and serve with a sprinkle of salt and Cuban Aïoli Sauce (page 122).

Cool fins, chrome galore and amazing shapes are commonplace on every street on the island

It's ironic that the flash 1950s American cars are iconically Cuban. Cool fins, chrome galore and amazing shapes are commonplace on every street on the island – an integral part of the time warp beloved of visiting photographers.

Classic cars are used for everyday transport, there are camiones dating back to 1929 still chugging along dusty country roads and delivering thousands of Cubans to work every day. Others work the public taxi route, taking people down set journeys for a few

coins. Every kind of pre-Revolution classic American creation a petrol-head could dream of fills the streets. Dodges, Studebakers, Chevys, Hudsons, Buicks, Mercurys, Pontiacs, Thunderbirds.

Many Cubans would rather something more modern – even a Lada, Skoda or Moskvitche would be considered more desirable. A few dull-looking modern machines roam the streets these days, but these are tourist taxis or cars reserved for the smattering of foreigners who call Cuba home.

Their continued use is more to do with the resourcefulness and maintenance skills of Cuban mechanics than the wizardry of American car manufacturers – most of these cars bit the dust Stateside years ago. On top of that, classic car parts which are easy to come by in the States are out of bounds for Cubans because of the US trade embargo. So Cubans make do with whatever they can.

In a country where the average monthly salary is $10–$15 (but accommodation, healthcare and education are free), a car is invaluable as a source of income. Their continued use has also come to be seen as a symbol of the Cuban ability to endure hard times – and keep effortlessly cool at the same time.

The phenomenon of Nuevo Latino has evolved in this fertile Cuban diaspora

As with any diasporic community, the Cubans who left in '59, and their direct descendants, mourn a country that doesn't exist anymore, and perpetuate habits which Cubans in Cuba wouldn't recognise as being particularly Cuban anymore. The exception to this, however, is their food, which has developed and flourished in other countries where ingredients are unrestricted and plentiful. Nuevo Latino (New Latin American cuisine), using different ingredients,

lighter dishes and exciting combinations has created an interest in Cuban cooking like never before. Miami, New York, London, Madrid and many other international cities now boast first-class Cuban restaurants. In spite of all these new creations, Cubans remain steadfastly loyal to their traditional dishes as well: Moros y Cristianos (page 108) and Tostones (page 103) are just two dishes that continue to feature on Cuban restaurant menus, wherever they may be.

Okra in Spicy Tomato and Garlic Sauce

Serves 4

The secret to this recipe is to rub the okra in coarse sea salt before cooking so that the salt draws out the excess liquid. It makes the okra much crunchier.

450 g okra, left whole
coarse sea salt

For the sauce
2 tablespoons olive oil
1 large Spanish onion, diced
4 garlic cloves, crushed
6 large tomatoes, skinned, de-seeded and chopped
1 fresh red chilli, de-seeded and finely chopped
1 tablespoon finely chopped fresh basil
1 teaspoon salt
freshly ground black pepper
a few torn basil leaves, to garnish

First of all, prepare the okra. Rub some coarse sea salt into the okra with your hands, making sure they are well rubbed. Set aside for 20 minutes – the salt will draw the liquid out of the okra. Rinse and pat dry.

Next, make the sauce. Heat the oil in a large saucepan, add the onion and cook over a moderate heat for 5 minutes until soft and golden. Add the garlic and cook for a further 2 minutes, stirring constantly. Stir in the tomatoes, chilli, basil, salt and pepper to taste and pour over 175 ml water. Bring to the boil, then reduce the heat to low and simmer for 5 minutes.

Add the salt-blanched okra to the pan and cook for 10–15 minutes, depending on the size of the okra, stirring occasionally.

Taste and adjust the seasoning. Transfer to a warmed serving dish, garnish with the torn basil leaves and serve immediately.

Moros y Cristianos

Serves 4–6

As the national dish of Cuba, this is treasured by all Cubans. Essentially, it is a mixture of black beans and rice, but each family has its own secret recipe. I have given this recipe my own secret ingredient – duck fat – but you can use olive oil instead.

The literal translation of Moros y Cristianos is 'the Moors and the Christians'. This refers to Medieval times in Spain when the Moors (Muslims) and the Christians lived side by side before the Spanish Inquisition. Black beans are native to Central and South America and rice was introduced to Cuba by the Spanish.

1 tablespoon duck fat, melted
  (or 1 tablespoon olive oil)
25 g bacon lardons
1 small onion, chopped
250 g long grain rice, cooked
125 g black beans, cooked (see page 102
  for method)
1 tablespoon finely chopped
  fresh parsley
salt and freshly ground black pepper
olive oil, to drizzle

Heat the duck fat in a large frying pan, add the bacon lardons and fry over a moderate heat for 5 minutes, or until they are golden brown. Reduce the heat to low, add the onion and cook for a further 5 minutes. Then stir in the rice and beans. Season with salt and pepper and cook for a few more minutes, until heated through. Serve in a bowl with the chopped parsley and a drizzle of olive oil.

Malanga Fritters

Makes 24

Malanga is one of the most popular vegetables in Cuba. In fact, in Cuba, a couple of potato-like vegetables are called malanga although they look quite different from one another. The more popular variety is long and shaped like a parsnip while the other variety is round in shape. When cooked, they have a nutty flavour and a starchy consistency. They are best sourced from Afro-Caribbean grocers.

1 kg malangas (cocoyam)
1 teaspoon salt
1 teaspoon garlic purée
salt and freshly ground black pepper
vegetable oil, for deep-frying

Immerse the malangas in a saucepan of boiling water. Add a teaspoon of salt and continue boiling for 15 minutes. Drain and, when the malanga are cool enough to handle, peel then grate into a mixing bowl.

Season the grated malanga with the garlic purée, a little more salt and some freshly ground black pepper.

Heat the oil in a heavy-based frying pan. When the oil is hot, drop tablespoons of the malanga mixture into the pan, a few at a time. Fry for 2–3 minutes, or until they are golden brown.

Remove with a slotted spoon and drain on kitchen paper. Keep warm while frying the remaining fritters.

Transfer to a warmed serving dish and serve immediately.

Latin Cheese Breads

Makes 30 little breads

These little breads were inspired by some that I ate in Brazil. If you find that they don't rise you can always add 1 tablespoon of yeast to the flour. Don't leave them out too long or they will harden. You can freeze them for a couple of months, baked or unbaked and stored in a container with greaseproof paper between each layer. They can then be cooked directly from frozen.

2 tablespoons softened butter
175 ml vegetable oil, plus a little
    more for rolling the balls
550 ml milk
575 g tapioca flour
2 free range organic eggs, beaten
340 g grated Edam cheese

Grease two large baking sheets with the butter.

Pour the oil and milk into a saucepan and bring to the boil over a moderate heat. Put the tapioca flour in a bowl, pour over the hot oil and milk mixture. Mix well with a wooden spoon. Set aside to stand for 10 minutes.

Preheat the oven to 180°C/Gas Mark 4.

Add the beaten eggs and Edam cheese to the flour and milk mixture, and mix well. (The mixture will be sticky and gooey.)

Rub your palms with a little oil and make 30 balls, each about 5 cm in diameter. Make sure that your hands are always lightly oiled when you are forming the balls.

Place on the buttered baking sheets and bake in the oven for 15–20 minutes, or until the tops are light brown.

There is racial harmony, intermarrying and mixing in Cuba that is truly unique.

Cubans are Hispanics (largely Canarians, Galicians, Catalans and Asturians), mulattoes and Afro-Cubans, whose ancestors were slaves. The population was ethnically and economically divided before the Revolution, but Castro's Cuba has opened up education and employment to all Cubans, and housing has been equitably distributed. There is a kind of racial harmony, intermarrying and mixing in Cuba that is truly unique.

A much smaller number of Cubans abroad are of African descent. The majority of Cuban exiles in Miami are of Spanish origin – the descendants of the wealthy Cubans who left

at the time of the Revolution. There is also a Chinese community, descended from Chinese labourers brought to Cuba at the end of the 19th century, to work alongside the African slaves in the cane fields. Cuba's Chinese boom ended when, from 1959, Castro seized private businesses, sending tens of thousands of Chinese fleeing over the Florida Straits.

There is a small surviving Indian community, mainly in El Oriente, consisting of Taino people, who originally came from Puerto Rico. In the mid 19th century, immigrant Arabs used Cuba as a transit point to the USA, but by the 1930s the Arab population numbered over 30,000. Today, like many others, they have intermarried and become part of the Cuban tapestry.

Finally, there is a small Jewish community of about 1,000 living in Havana; more then 150,000 Jews came to Havana before the Revolution, most fleeing Nazi Germany; the majority left after Castro came to power in 1959. This largely Hispanic-Afro mélange, sometimes spiced with Amerindian, Chinese and Arab notes, has created a strikingly beautiful race of people and a unique cuisine.

SAUCES
AND DRESSINGS

Creole Garlic Sauce (Mojo Criollo)

Serves 4

The versatility of a mojo, a staple seasoning in Cuba that can be used as a dip, marinade or sauce, is evident in its wide use in Cuban cuisine. This recipe is very zesty and a great accompaniment to both chicken and pork.

3 garlic cloves, crushed
1 teaspoon salt
1 large onion, very thinly sliced
125 ml sour orange juice (from Seville oranges), or use a mixture of half orange, half lemon juice
2 tablespoons lime juice
2 teaspoons extra virgin olive oil

Using a pestle and mortar, crush the garlic with the salt to form a paste. Mix in the onions and citric juices. Leave to sit at room temperature for 1 hour to allow the flavours to develop.

Heat the olive oil over a medium heat until very hot. Add the garlic mixture, sauté for a few seconds and serve immediately over the desired dish.

Classic Béchamel Sauce

Makes 500 ml

500 ml milk
a few parsley stalks
1 bay leaf
a pinch of powdered mace or nutmeg
1 teaspoon whole black peppercorns
12 small onions, sliced
45 g butter
45 g plain flour
salt and freshly ground black pepper

Put the milk, parsley stalks, bay leaf, mace or nutmeg, peppercorns and onions in a small saucepan. Place over a low heat for 5 minutes or until the milk begins to simmer. Remove from the heat and strain into a jug, discarding the flavourings.

Melt the butter gently over a low heat, being careful not to allow it to colour. Stir in the flour, increase the heat to medium and make a smooth, glossy paste (called a roux), stirring constantly.

Add the infused milk a little at a time, stirring constantly and ensuring that each addition of milk is fully incorporated into the roux mixture. When half the milk has been used, change to using a whisk and pour in the milk a little more quickly, whisking constantly.

Lower the heat and let the sauce cook for 5–10 minutes, whisking from time to time. Season with salt and pepper. If you are not using the sauce immediately, cover the top with some greaseproof paper to prevent a skin from forming.

Beurre Blanc (White Butter Sauce)

Makes approximately 250 g

This is a traditional French sauce and is the perfect accompaniment to grilled or roasted fish. Like Lobster Thermidor, this is part of the repertoire of international dishes used in Cuban cuisine.

2 banana shallots
375 ml white wine
a bunch of parsley
1 sprig of tarragon
4 tablespoons cream
100 g butter, chilled and diced
salt and freshly ground black pepper

Using a saucepan, add the shallots, cover with the white wine and then add the parsley and tarragon.

Bring to the boil over a moderate heat and continue to simmer for about 6 minutes or until the white wine has reduced by half. Strain the sauce through a sieve into a clean pan. Stir in the cream, bring it back to the boil, and cook for a further 5 minutes. Whisk in the butter. Season to taste with salt and pepper. Set aside and keep warm.

For best results, use right away since it does not store as well as other sauces.

Chunky Tomato Sauce

Makes 500 ml

2 tablespoons extra virgin olive oil
2 medium onions, roughly chopped
3 garlic cloves, finely chopped
600 g vine tomatoes, skinned, peeled and de-seeded, then roughly chopped
2 tablespoons tomato purée
1 tablespoon torn fresh basil leaves
salt and freshly ground pepper

Heat the olive oil over a moderate heat. Add the onions and garlic and sweat for 6 minutes, stirring occasionally. Stir in the tomatoes, tomato purée and basil leaves. Cover with a lid, reduce the heat to low and cook for 20 minutes, stirring occasionally. Season to taste. Chill or freeze until needed.

Hot Tomato Sauce

Makes 800 ml

900 g ripe tomatoes, skinned, halved
    and de-seeded
10 g fresh thyme leaves
2 tablespoons extra virgin olive oil
2 teaspoons salt
freshly ground black pepper
2 medium onions, sliced
4 garlic cloves, crushed
1 jalapeño chilli pepper, chopped
1 x 400 g tin plum tomatoes
2 teaspoons caster sugar
1 teaspoon Encona hot sauce, to taste

Preheat the oven to 200°C/Gas Mark 6.

Arrange the tomatoes, facing upwards, on
two large baking sheets. Sprinkle over the
thyme, a drizzle of olive oil and the salt and
season with pepper. Roast for 30 minutes
or until soft. Set aside to cool.

Heat the remaining olive oil in a non-stick
pan and sweat the onions with the garlic
and jalapeño chilli pepper for 8 minutes or
until soft. Add the tinned tomatoes, then
stir in the roasted tomatoes and sugar.
Cover with a lid and cook over a low heat
for 1 hour.

Remove the pan from the heat and allow to
cool slightly. Strain the sauce through a
sieve, season to taste, then add the Encona
hot sauce for a bit of heat (as much or as
little as you prefer). Chill or freeze until
needed.

Oregano and Sour Orange Mojo

Makes approximately 600 ml

This is a variation on the traditional Mojo
Criollo (page 116). It can be used for
marinating meat and poultry before cooking,
as a sauce whilst cooking or as a dressing
after cooking. It can be stored in the fridge
for several days.

100 ml extra virgin olive oil
1 onion, finely chopped
10 garlic cloves, thinly sliced
½ teaspoon fresh oregano leaves,
    finely chopped
1 teaspoon ground cumin
½ teaspoon salt and freshly ground
    black pepper
100 ml freshly squeezed orange juice
275 ml freshly squeezed lime juice
150 ml water
2 tablespoons fresh coriander leaves,
    finely chopped

Heat 2 tablespoons of the olive oil in a
saucepan over a low heat. Add the onion
and garlic and cook for 5–7 minutes,
stirring constantly, until soft and golden
but not brown.

Add the remaining ingredients, with the
exception of the fresh coriander. Bring the
sauce to the boil, remove from the heat and
set aside to cool to room temperature. Stir
in the coriander and serve warm.

House Salad Dressing

Makes 500 ml

100 ml red wine vinegar
100 ml red wine
1 tablespoon Dijon mustard
1 teaspoon Worcestershire sauce
½ teaspoon salt
2 tablespoons chopped onions
1 teaspoon chopped garlic
a generous pinch of dried herbs
300 ml extra virgin olive oil

Using a hand-held blender, blitz together all the ingredients, except the olive oil. Gradually beat in the olive oil. This will make enough to keep in the refrigerator for several weeks.

Caesar Salad Dressing

Makes approximately 300 ml

1 garlic clove, crushed
2 free range organic egg yolks
2 anchovies
100 ml sherry vinegar
2 heaped tablespoons freshly grated
    Parmesan cheese
3 drops of Worcestershire sauce
200 ml olive oil
salt and freshly ground black pepper

Whisk together the garlic, egg yolks, anchovies, sherry vinegar, Parmesan cheese and Worcestershire sauce until thoroughly blended. Slowly whisk in the olive oil. Season to taste with salt and pepper. Use immediately.

Chimmichurri Dressing

Makes 1/2 litre

1 bunch flat leaf parsley,
    picked and finely chopped
5 garlic cloves, finely chopped
½ teaspoon freshly ground
    black pepper
2 teaspoons sea salt
½ teaspoon finely chopped fresh
    red chilli, de-seeded
2 tablespoons picked oregano leaves
3 tablespoons finely chopped
    red onions
3 tablespoons sherry vinegar
zest and juice of 2 lemons
300 ml extra virgin olive oil

Mix all the ingredients together in a bowl
and use as desired.

Cuban Aïoli Sauce

Serves 4

8 garlic cloves
2 free range organic egg yolks
a small pinch of powdered saffron
juice of 1 lemon
450 ml olive oil
salt and freshly ground black pepper

Crush the garlic in a bowl. Whisk in the egg
yolks, saffron and lemon juice. Drizzle in
the olive oil, a little at a time, whisking
constantly. The mixture should thicken
gradually. Season with salt and pepper.

Béchamel Sauce for Lobster Thermidor

Serves 6

125 g butter
2 onions, diced
1 celery stalk, diced
125 g flour
1 litre milk
salt and freshly ground black pepper
a pinch of grated nutmeg
a pinch of cayenne pepper
180 ml double cream
2 free range organic egg yolks
2 tablespoons grated Parmesan cheese

Melt the butter in a saucepan over a low
heat, then add the onions and celery. Cover
and sweat for 5–7 minutes or until soft and
translucent but not brown. Add the flour
and cook for a further 2–3 minutes, stirring
constantly. Slowly add the milk, still
stirring, then increase the heat and bring
the mixture to the boil. Reduce the heat to
low and simmer for 15 minutes.

Add salt, pepper, the nutmeg, cayenne
pepper, cream, egg yolks and Parmesan
cheese. Cook for a further 3–5 minutes on a
low heat until the sauce is thick enough to
coat the back of a spoon.

DESSERTS

Coconut Shortbread

Makes 30

250 g butter, cut into cubes
   at room temperature
110 g icing sugar, plus a little extra
   for dusting
1 teaspoon vanilla essence
300 g plain flour
30 g desiccated coconut

Preheat the oven to 150°C/Gas Mark 2.

Line two baking sheets with non-stick
baking paper.

Beat the butter, sugar and vanilla essence
with a wooden spoon until smooth and
light. Mix in the flour and coconut. Wrap
in clingfilm and rest in the fridge for
30 minutes.

Roll heaped teaspoons of the shortbread
dough into balls and place on the baking
sheets.

Bake for 10 minutes, remove from the oven,
transfer to a wire rack and let stand for a
further 5 minutes. Dust with extra icing
sugar.

Acai and Banana Sorbet

Serves 4

Acai (pronounced asa-i) is a Brazilian berry
that looks similar to a small grape. It is
considered to be one of nature's superfoods
and is loaded with antioxidants,
anthocyanins, amino acids, essential omegas,
fibre and protein. The juice and pulp of acai
fruits (*Euterpe oleracea*) are frequently used
in various juice blends, smoothies, sodas and
other beverages, as well as ice creams and
sorbets. The berries are available through
www.magaberries.co.uk

100 g acai berries
50 g blackcurrants
150 g ripe bananas
zest and juice of 1 lemon
70 g caster sugar
1 free range organic egg white

Blend the acai berries, blackcurrants,
bananas, lemon zest and juice and sugar
until puréed. Sieve the purée and freeze
overnight.

The next day, break the frozen purée into
pieces and put it back into the liquidizer
with the egg white. Blend together on the
pulse setting for 2 minutes until smooth
but still frozen.

Serve immediately with Coconut
Shortbread (left).

Caramelized Chilled Vanilla Rice Pudding

Serves 8

125 ml double cream
300 ml milk
2½ tablespoons caster sugar
100 g pudding rice
1 vanilla pod, split lengthways,
   seeds scooped out, seeds and
   pod reserved
1 cinnamon stick
1 teaspoon ground cinnamon
125 ml whipping cream, whipped
8 tablespoons soft dark brown sugar

Put the double cream, milk and sugar in a saucepan and bring to the boil over a moderate heat. Add the rice, vanilla pod and seeds, cinnamon stick and ground cinnamon. Reduce the heat and simmer very slowly for 20 minutes until cooked.

Remove from the heat and transfer to a bowl. Set aside to cool and when cold, chill in the fridge for a couple of hours.

To serve, fold the whipped cream into the chilled rice. Place in a small ring mould. Dust with the brown sugar and place under a very hot grill for 2–3 minutes until the sugar has melted.

Almond and Lemon Egg Custard Tart

Serves 6–8

8 free range organic egg yolks
75 g caster sugar
zest and juice of 2 lemons
500 g whipping cream
100 g almonds, toasted
20 cm sweet pastry case
a little grated nutmeg

Preheat the oven to 180°C/Gas Mark 4.

To make the custard, combine the egg yolks with the sugar in a bowl until pale golden. Add the lemon zest and juice and set aside.

Place the whipping cream in a saucepan and bring to the boil. Pour a little of the boiled cream into the custard, mixing a little, then add the remaining cream, stirring constantly. Stir in half of the almonds.

Fill the pastry case with the custard mixture, sprinkle over a little grated nutmeg and the remaining almonds.

Place in the oven and bake for 15 minutes. Remove from the oven and set aside to cool before serving.

Religion in Cuba is another reflection of the island's complex identity

Since 1992, restrictions have been eased on the churches; the Pope even paid a visit in 1998, despite 80 per cent of priests leaving after the Revolution when Cuba became officially atheist. Traditionally a Catholic country before 1959, its beliefs have intermingled and transmogrified with West African beliefs, also creating Santeria, which developed out of the traditions of

the Yoruba, one of the African peoples who were brought to Cuba between the 16th and 19th centuries. Originally it was a way for slaves to retain their original beliefs, while appearing to practise Catholicism. It stuck and spread.

Cuba's patron saint, La Virgen de la Caridiad del Cobre, Our Lady of Charity, is also the Santeria goddess Ochun. Other Christian saints have also merged with the orishas (deities) of the Santeros, and those of other cults coming from Africa.

Chilled Tapioca Pudding with Ice Cream and a Sesame Seed Biscuit

Serves 10

Tapioca is one of my favourite ingredients – one that I think is much maligned. This recipe will cancel any thoughts you may have about school dinners!

200 ml double cream
400 ml milk
1 tablespoon butter
50 g caster sugar
50 g tapioca
1 cinnamon stick
1 vanilla pod
a little grated nutmeg, to taste
100 ml whipped cream
10 Sesame Seed Tuille (right), to serve
10 balls of ice cream, to serve

Bring the double cream, milk, butter and sugar to the boil. Add the tapioca, cinnamon, vanilla pod and nutmeg. Reduce the heat to low and simmer very slowly for 20 minutes or until cooked.

Remove the cinnamon and vanilla and set the mixture aside to cool. When cool, chill in the fridge for 30 minutes. When chilled, fold the whipped cream into the tapioca.

To serve: place a small ring of tapioca in the centre of the plate, place one tuille on top and cover with a ball of ice cream.

Sesame Seed Tuille

Makes approximately 30

100 ml orange juice
zest of 2 oranges
200 g icing sugar
60 g flour
125 g sesame seeds
120 g melted butter

Mix all the ingredients together in a bowl and place in the fridge for 2 hours.

Preheat the oven to 180°C/Gas Mark 4. Line two baking sheets with silicone paper. Drop teaspoonfuls of the mixture on to the baking sheets, leaving plenty of room in between each one.

Bake for 15–20 minutes or until the tuille are golden brown. Remove from the oven and set aside to cool and harden before serving. These will store well in an airtight container for a few days.

Coconut Caramel Flan

Makes 4

250 ml milk
4 tablespoons cream
100 ml tinned coconut milk
1 vanilla pod, split lengthways and
  seeds scraped out
4 or 5 large free range organic egg yolks
100 g caster sugar

For the caramel
100 g caster sugar
2 tablespoons water

Preheat the oven to 160°C/Gas Mark 3.

Put the milk, cream, coconut milk and vanilla pod in a saucepan and bring to the boil.

Beat the egg yolks with the sugar until light and creamy.

Mix one third of the milk mixture into the eggs. Then add this to the rest of the milk mixture, stirring well. Leave to stand.

To make the caramel, put the sugar and water in a heavy-based saucepan, place over a high heat and boil for 6–8 minutes or until dark caramel in colour. Cool slightly, then pour into the base of four ramekins, each approximately 7.5 cm, to form a thin 0.5 cm layer.

Leave to set for 2 minutes, then pour over the milk and egg mixture. Fill a roasting tin halfway up with boiling water and place the ramekins in the water. Cook in the pre-heated oven for 25 minutes or until set. Remove from the oven, leave to cool for half an hour and refrigerate for two hours.

To serve, run a knife around the edges of the ramekins and tip out upside down on to a plate.

Bitter Chocolate Cheesecake with Kumquats in Ginger

Serves 8

175 g digestive biscuits
175 g ginger snap biscuits
50 g butter
375 g cream cheese
150 g caster sugar, plus another
    2 tablespoons
3 free range organic eggs, yolks
    and whites separated
2 tablespoons flour
zest and juice of 2 lemons
225 g good quality (55–58%)
    dark chocolate, melted
100 ml whipping cream, whipped,
    to serve
a few sprigs of fresh mint, to serve

For kumquats in ginger
100 g kumquats
100 g caster sugar
25 g freshly grated root ginger
100 ml water

Put the digestive and ginger snap biscuits in a food processor, add the butter and blitz until the mixture turns into crumbs. Pour the biscuit crumb mixture into the bottom of a 23 cm loose-bottomed cake tin and press down with your fingertips to make an even layer.

Preheat the oven to 160°C/Gas Mark 3. Beat the cream cheese until smooth, then beat in the 150 g caster sugar until the mixture is light and fluffy. Fold in the egg yolks, flour, lemon zest and juice and finally the melted chocolate.

In a separate mixing bowl, whisk the egg whites until peaks start to form. Add the remaining 2 tablespoons of sugar and continue to whisk until stiff. Fold into the cream cheese mixture, then spoon over the biscuit base.

Stand the cake tin in a roasting tin filled with boiling water two-thirds up the sides and bake in the oven for 60 minutes or until the cheesecake has set. Allow to cool then refrigerate for at least 4 hours.

Wash the kumquats and cut widthways into 0.5-cm thick slices. Put the sugar and grated ginger in a saucepan, add the water and bring to a boil. Add the kumquats and continue boiling for 10 minutes. Remove from the heat and leave to cool for 1 hour. Place back on the heat and re-boil once again for a further 10 minutes, then leave to cool for another hour. Repeat this once more then refrigerate until needed.

To serve, slice the cake and serve each portion with a tablespoon of the whipped cream, topped with a fan of the candied kumquats and a sprig of fresh mint.

Sticky Banana Puddings with Rum Toffee Sauce

Makes 8 puddings

For the banana puddings
225 g dried bananas, diced and soaked
    overnight in water
375 ml water
1 teaspoon bicarbonate of soda
50 g butter
350 g caster sugar
2 free range organic eggs
175 g flour
1 teaspoon baking powder

For the rum toffee sauce
500 g caster sugar
125 g butter, softened
375 ml double cream
4 tablespoons rum

Preheat the oven to 190°C/Gas Mark 5.

Drain the bananas. Put in a saucepan and cover with the water. Boil for 20 minutes, or until soft. Stir in the bicarbonate of soda. Remove from the heat and set aside.

In a separate mixing bowl, cream the butter and sugar together, until light and fluffy. Add the eggs slowly, then mix in the flour, baking powder and the bananas.

Spoon the banana pudding mixture into eight ramekins and place in a deep roasting tin. Fill the tin with enough boiling water to come halfway up the sides. Place in the oven and cook for 50 minutes or until the puddings are firm to the touch.

While the puddings are cooking, make the rum toffee sauce. Place the sugar in a heavy-based saucepan over a moderate to low heat. Slowly melt the sugar until it is totally liquid, tipping the pan constantly. Cook the melted sugar for a few minutes until it is light brown. Remove from the heat and whisk in the softened butter.

Stir in the double cream and rum. Return the saucepan to the heat and cook for a further 10 minutes, or until the mixture has reduced and is thick enough to coat the back of a spoon.

Remove the roasting tin from the oven. Run a knife around the edge of each pudding and turn out on to a serving plate. Leave to cool slightly and serve with the rum toffee sauce drizzled over.

Fairtrade Spiced Chocolate and Almond Cake

Makes 1 x 20 cm cake

I always try to use the very best ingredients when I cook and, where possible, buy produce that will benefit the source. By buying Fairtrade chocolate, I know that some of the money will filter back to the producers. This recipe can be served for tea or as a dessert served with fruit and lashings of clotted cream or ice-cream.

2½ tablespoons Fairtrade cocoa powder, plus a little extra to dust the cake tin
8 free range organic eggs, yolks and whites separated
230 g caster sugar
130 g ground almonds
3½ tablespoons plain flour, sieved
1½ tablespoons ground mixed spice
415 g Fairtrade dark chocolate, melted
230 g butter, softened

Preheat the oven to 170°C/Gas Mark 3. Grease a 20 cm loose-bottomed cake tin and dust well with Fairtrade cocoa powder.

Cream together the egg yolks and half the sugar, until light and fluffy.

In a separate bowl, mix the ground almonds, flour and mixed spice together. In another bowl, whisk the egg whites with the remaining sugar, until soft peaks form.

Mix the melted chocolate with the butter and then fold into the egg yolk mixture. Then fold in the whipped egg whites, starting with one third of the mixture, followed by the rest. Gradually and lastly, fold in the flour mixture, making sure that the mixture remains light and aerated. Pour into the cake tin.

Bake for approximately 1 hour, or until the cake becomes firm and springy to the touch when lightly pressed in the middle.

Leave to cool, slice and serve with clotted cream or ice-cream.

Praline Coffee Soufflé

Serves 2

If you can't find praline paste, use Nutella instead.

3 free range organic eggs, yolks and
    whites separated
2½ tablespoons caster sugar
2 leaves gelatine
1 tablespoon instant coffee
125 ml double cream, whipped, plus
    2 spoonfuls for garnish
3 tablespoons praline paste or Nutella
2 small sprigs of mint, to garnish

You will need two ramekin dishes. Wrap a cylinder or collar of greaseproof paper round each one and secure with tape. Make sure the paper comes at least 5 cm above the top of the ramekins.

Beat the egg yolks with the sugar until pale yellow. Melt the gelatine in 4 tablespoons hot water in a mixing bowl, then stir in the coffee. Beat in the egg and sugar mixture then fold in the whipped cream and praline paste.

In a separate bowl, whisk the egg whites until they form stiff peaks. Fold into the soufflé mixture, then carefully pour into the prepared ramekins. Leave to set in the fridge for 1 hour.

To serve, carefully remove the paper collars, place a spoonful of whipped cream on the top of each soufflé and garnish with a couple of mint leaves.

One of the best ways to experience Cuban food is to have a meal at a paladare

A paladare is a family-run and -owned restaurant operating from a home. In the mid 1990s Castro gave permission for people to provide paying diners with home-cooked food as part of his introduction to private enterprise. The government has imposed quite a few restrictions, which change quite often. Originally, only family members were meant to work there and restaurants can serve no more than 12 people at a time. They also have to pay substantial taxes and keep detailed records, which are frequently checked.

COCKTAILS

History of El Floridita

Founded in Havana in the early 20th century, El Floridita was a place where history was made with regulars across the years, including luminaries such as Ernest Hemingway, Spencer Tracy, Gary Cooper, Noel Coward and Errol Flynn and more recently, Naomi Campbell, Paco Rabanne, Jack Nicholson and Bruce Willis.

Under the supervision of the legendary master bartender, Constante, El Floridita became known in the early 1900s as Havana's 'cathedral of cocktails' with the frozen daiquiri being its most famous creation.

The origins of the daiquiri cocktail are still debated. Although Constante is renowned for his frozen daiquri, the original straight daiquiri was allegedly invented by Jennings S. Cox, a mining manager in Southeast Cuba who named it after the nearest town to his mine, Daiquiri. Constante took the cocktail, blended it with shaved ice and the famous 'frozen daiquiri' was

'He had drunk double frozen daiquiris, the great ones that Constante made, that had no taste of alcohol and felt, as you drank them, the way downhill glacier skiing feels running through powder snow and, after the sixth and eighth, felt like downhill glacier skiing feels when you are running unroped...'

Islands In The Stream,
ERNEST HEMINGWAY

born. Today, El Floridita is recognized worldwide as the home of the daiquiri.

The story of the famous El Floridita cocktail starts at the outbreak of the First World War, when the cantinero (the words barman or bartender were not yet in use) Constantino Ribbalaigua Vert made his debut. Constante, as everyone called him, showed unceasing dedication and professionalism towards his work. El Floridita became a college for cantineros and even today, bartenders from all over the world continue to make their pilgrimage to sharpen their skills.

Ernest Hemingway (above left, next to Spencer Tracy) fell in love with Havana in the early thirties and by 1940 had become a regular fixture at a corner seat at the bar in El Floridita. Constante created a special cocktail for him – the Papa Doble – a double daiquiri with the addition of a little grapefruit juice but without sugar, served blended with crushed ice.

If you want to take cocktail-making a little more seriously, then you will need to acquire a few pieces of equipment such as a sharp knife, a metal ice bucket, ice tongs, a measure (it's best to have two – one twice the size of the other), a cocktail shaker, a bar glass with a strainer and a long-handled bar spoon that is used for mixing and layering both alcoholic and non-alcoholic drinks (a bar spoon holds about 5 ml of liquid – the same as a teaspoon). You will also need a wooden muddler, which is used to crush solid items such as mint or ginger before you add the other ingredients.

All these cocktails serve 1

Sugar Syrup
Makes 300 ml

300 ml water
300 ml white sugar

Place the water and sugar in a saucepan and place over a low heat. Heat slowly until all the sugar has dissolved. Cool before using.

Daiquiri (Classic)

50 ml light-style Cuban rum (Cubay or Elements 8 Platinum)
15 ml freshly squeezed lime juice
5 ml sugar syrup (above)

Shake all the ingredients with cubed ice and strain into a chilled Martini glass.

Frozen Daiquiri

Constante took the Daiquiri a step further by mixing the ingredients in a blender with a few drops of Maraschino liqueur and some crushed ice. This blended drink created what was to become one of Cuba's most famous drinks – the Frozen Daiquiri.

50 ml light-style Cuban Rum, or something like Santa Teresa Claro from Venezuela
15 ml freshly squeezed lime juice
5 ml sugar syrup (left)
10 ml Maraschino liqueur

Pour all the ingredients into a blender with a scoop of crushed ice and blend until frappé, then pour into a chilled Martini glass.

Rhubarb and Honey Daiquiri

50 ml Appleton Estate V/X (Jamaican rum)
50 ml rhubarb purée
12.5 ml honey
10 ml freshly squeezed lime juice
some fresh honeycomb, to garnish
a stick of candied rhubarb, to garnish

Blend all the ingredients (except those for
the garnish) together on crushed ice. Use a
pulsing action to ensure that the honey is
fully integrated with the other ingredients.
Pour into a hurricane glass. Garnish with
some honeycomb and a stick of candied
rhubarb.

The Mojito

8–12 fresh mint leaves, plus a sprig
   to garnish
12.5 ml sugar syrup (opposite)
25 ml freshly squeezed lime juice
50 ml Havana Club Anejo
soda, to fill

Churn the mint, sugar syrup and lime juice
in a tall glass with some ice. Add the rum
more ice and top with a soda spritz.
Garnish with a sprig of mint.

Pineapple and Sage Mojito
A new twist to the classic Mojito!

4 sage leaves
10 ml sugar syrup (page 144)
50 ml special-aged rum
15 ml freshly squeezed lime juice
25 ml sage-infused pineapple purée
a dash of soda

Muddle (see below) the sage and sugar syrup in a tall glass. Pour in the rest of the ingredients, except the soda and a scoop of crushed ice. Churn with a bar spoon to mix and add a little more ice before topping with soda water.

To muddle… is to combine ingredients together in the bottom of a mixing glass using a small bat-shaped wooden pestle called a muddler. The large, rounded end is first used to mash the ingredients and release the flavours. Then the other thinner and flatter end is used to mix the ingredients together.

Floridita

50 ml Havana Club Anejo Especial
20 ml sweet vermouth
5 ml crème de cacao white
a dash of grenadine
a dash of freshly squeezed lime juice
a lime wedge, to garnish

Shake all the ingredients together, except the lime wedge, and double strain into a chilled Martini glass. Garnish with a lime wedge.

Cosa Nuestra

40 ml aged rum
2 bar spoons of maple syrup
25 ml vintage port
20 ml apple juice
a lemon twist, to garnish

Stir the rum and maple syrup with a bar spoon in a mixing glass until the syrup dissolves. Pour over the port and some rock ice and continue stirring for about 30 seconds. Add a little more ice and the apple juice. Stir some more then pour into a chilled Martini glass and garnish with a lemon twist.

Blackberry El Presidente

50 ml 7-year-old rum
25 ml sweet vermouth
15 ml blackberry purée
a dash of bitters
a dash of dry vermouth
a twist of lemon, to garnish

Stir all the ingredients, except the lemon, on rock ice and strain into a chilled small Martini glass. Garnish with a twist of lemon.

Ciruela Picante

1 plum, chopped,
    plus 3 slices, to garnish
10 ml vanilla liqueur
10 ml freshly squeezed lime juice
2 bar spoons of passionfruit purée
50 ml vanilla-infused aged rum
10 ml spiced rum

Muddle (see page 146) the chopped plum in a tall glass. Add the vanilla liqueur, lime juice and passionfruit purée. Churn with a scoop of crushed ice. Add the rums and churn again. Garnish with the plum slices.

Caramelo Pomelo

6–8 red grapes,
    plus two grapes for garnish
12.5 ml maple syrup
12.5 ml freshly squeezed lime juice
50 ml special-aged rum

Muddle (see page 146) the grapes in a highball glass. Pour in the maple syrup and lime juice. Stir again until the syrup has dissolved. Add some crushed ice and the rum, then churn. Add a little more crushed ice and then churn some more. Garnish with a couple of grapes.

All Cubans are issued with a rationing book...

All Cubans are issued with a rationing book, *Libreta de Abastecimiento* (supplies booklet) each year. This is Cuba's version of the welfare state – a lesson for many governments who should provide food rather than money. The vast majority of families rely on this for food purchases. Most of the products are distributed at the local bodega (convenience stores that specialize in ration distribution) and local carneceria (meat stores).

It was first introduced in 1962 and the government's objective was to ensure that each citizen received a minimum supply of food each month, regardless of his or her social and economic status. It also recognizes that the rations that are available by the system are not sufficient to provide adequate sustenance alone.

The Government stresses that other items can also be bought on the free markets and supermarkets and stores but the reality is these prices are unaffordable for the average salary. Prices in the ration book are at least 20 times lower than those on the free market.

An example of the standard allowance in the libreta per person per month:

rice 6 lb	
beans 20 oz	
white refined sugar 3 lb	
dark unrefined sugar 3 lb	
milk (only children under 7 years of age 1 litre per day)	
12 eggs (only from September through December)	
potatoes/bananas 15 lb	
1 bread roll per day	

Meat products are distributed every 15 days and vary between fish, beef, ground beef (usually mixed with soy) sausage, ham and chicken.

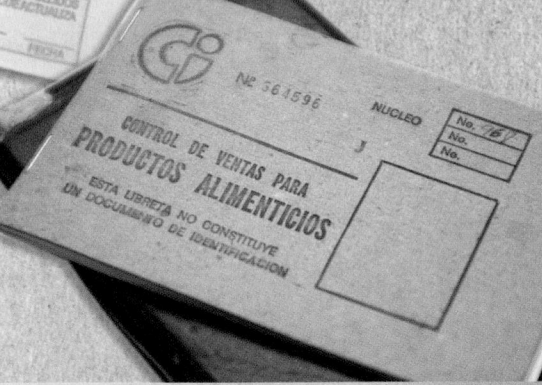

GLOSSARY

Acai – a Brazilian berry original from the Amazon Region. Loaded with antioxidants, anthocyanins (approximately 20 times the amount in red wine), amino acids, essential omegas, fibres and protein, the juice and pulp of acai fruits are used in juice blends, smoothies, and other beverages.

Annatto – also known as achiote, this is sold in the form of brick red seeds or a powder. It is often used as a colouring agent, or as a cheaper substitute for saffron.

Bananas – contain three natural sugars – sucrose, fructose and glucose – combined with fibre. Bananas may also be dried and eaten as a snack

food. Dried bananas are also ground into banana flour. Banana leaves are used for wrapping foods for steaming, such as tamales, fish and seafood.

Banana shallots – larger and much longer than other shallots, hence their name.

Basil leaf – a tender low-growing herb that is grown as a perennial in Cuba and other warm climates. The flavour is like anise, with a strong, pungent, sweet smell.

Beans – black, turtle, frijoles negros, red, white, butter. All these beans are an essential part of the Cuban kitchen. The flavour of each variety of beans is distinct, but they all share a wholesome, earthy taste. Black beans make up part of the rations provided by the government.

Calabaza/calabasa/West Indian or green pumpkin – a variety of squash commonly eaten in Latin America, the Philippines, and the Caribbean. About the same size as a pumpkin, with a green or yellow skin, it has a firm-textured flesh and a sweet flavour.

Caper – the pickled flower buds of the caper bush, their tangy, bitter flavour adds piquancy to many sauces and condiments with a Spanish or Latin American origin.

Cashew – an evergreen tree and shrub native to the Caribbean. It bears a tart reddish, pear-shaped cashew apple, from the bottom of which grows the kidney-shaped nut. It is usually eaten roasted.

Celeriac – has a tough, ridged, outer surface, which is usually cut off before use, because it is not smooth enough to peel. It has the flavour of celery, so it is often used on its own or as a flavouring in soups and stews; it can also be mashed or used in casseroles, gratins and baked dishes.

Chayote – a member of the pumpkin family, chayote is pear-shaped, and usually a light green with a slightly prickly skin. The texture is crisp with a delicate flavour similar to courgette but subtler. It is best when young and firm. It can be eaten raw and is delicious in salads.

Chicharrones – fried pork crackling sold as snacks in Cuba.

Chimmichurri – a pesto-like condiment, it is made from a base of parsley and other herbs, garlic, olive oil and sometimes sherry. Used as a dressing with meat.

Chocolate and cocoa – the presence of cocoa in Cuba dates from 1748. At the beginning of the 1800s there was large scale exportation of cocoa and coffee. The cocoa tree was introduced to be cultivated and didn't grow in the wild. The only region where cultivation continues today is in Baracoa, in the south eastern tip of the island.

Chorizo – a lightly smoked Spanish sausage of chopped pork, seasoned with garlic, sweet red pepper and hot paprika.

Cilantro – this pungent-tasting plant is part of the parsley family and is often confused with flat leaf parsley. It is very popular in all Latin American kitchens.

Cinnamon – a spice made from the bark of the cinnamon tree. It is used as a flavouring for sweet and savoury dishes. Used extensively in Cuban desserts. Sold as a bark or ground as a powder.

Coconut and coconut milk – the fruit of the *Cocos nucifera*. Both the milk and cream are used in cooking and for making cocktails such as pina colada.

Coffee – Cuban coffee is almost as popular as its rum. Served in small cups, it is a type of expresso, which is sweetened as it is brewed. Deliciously strong and aromatic.

Congris – rice and beans cooked together in a similar way to Moros y Cristianos. Sometimes red beans are used instead of black beans.

Corn – corn grows in 'ears', each of which is covered in rows of kernels that are then protected by the silk-like threads called 'corn husk' and encased in a husk. The corn silk is used as a casing for tamales, which are filled with a mixture of ground corn, seasoning and a variety of meats.

Culantro – sometimes called long coriander or recao, this herb is native to Latin America and is related to cilantro. It has tall, stiff, serrated leaves with a prominent central ridge and a more penetrating aroma than cilantro, with an assertive sage-citrus flavour.

Cumin seed – a yellowish-brownish oval-shaped seed of a plant of the parsley family, which is sold whole or ground and used in many Cuban dishes and sauces.

Escabeche – this literally means 'pickled' and is used to describe a Spanish or Portuguese method of cooking. Most often used with fish which is first cooked then pickled in a vinegar marinade.

Farofa/gari – grated yuca or cassava, dried and toasted. Used as a starch, in the same way as rice.

Garbanzo beans – also known as chickpeas, they have a delicious nut-like taste and buttery texture. Generally sold dried, the beans need to be soaked overnight and drained before cooking.

Guanabana – also called Sugar Apple and Custard Apple. When ripe, the green fruit turns greenish-

yellow. Inside, the white juicy flesh has a cottony texture and a highly aromatic, vanilla-like flavour. Used for drinks and ice cream.

Guava – a yellow-skinned oval or round tropical fruit, with white to pink flesh. This fruit is eaten raw or stewed, and often made into jams, stews and guava paste – a rich, solid preserve sold in blocks and often eaten with fresh cheese. The combination is called Romeo y Juliet in Cuba.

Langosta – Cuba is renowned for its langosta, which are spiny lobsters or crayfish. They have much more meat in their body than other lobsters but do not have claws. Cuba is unique among major lobster-producing countries because of its combination of strong central control and the absence of standardisation and mechanization in fishing gear.

Lime – brought to the Caribbean by early European settlers, the lime has become one of the most important ingredients in Cuban cooking. It is used in most dishes, from fish to poultry and

meat, as a flavouring for vegetables, desserts, sauces and as a main ingredient in the famous Cuban cocktails.

Malanga/yautia, also know as tannia, tannier, cocoyam and taro – a root vegetable (actually a corm, a compressed underground stem) resembling a yam, that was first cultivated in tropical America in the mid 1800s. With more than 40 species, the various species of malanga or yautia, are popular in Cuba and Puerto Rico. Malanga has more flavour than most other starchy tropical tubers, and its taste is earthy, and has been described as more like nuts than potatoes.

Mammee apple – also known as the San Domingo apricot and South American apricot. An evergreen tree of the family Clusiaceae, whose fruit is edible.

Mango – with many different varieties of mango in Cuba this fruit has experienced a revival in production due to the Urban Agricultural Movement. Generally eaten raw when ripe, it is also puréed as a drink or used in ice cream and other desserts.

Moros y Cristianos – this is regarded as the national dish of Cuba and literally translated means Moors and Christians, referring to the black beans and white rice, which are cooked together.

Mint – also called Yerba Buena, mint is used extensively in Cuban cooking and in the famous Mojito cocktail.

Mirin – a Japanese cooking wine, sometimes used in sauces in Neuvo Latino dishes.

Mojo – a Cuban seasoning of garlic, olive oil and sour (Seville) oranges, often with the addition of different herbs. There are many variations and it can be used as a dip, a marinade or a sauce.

Morcilla sausage – a Spanish-style blood sausage (black pudding) eaten in many Latin American countries. It is generally made with pig's blood, paprika and rice.

Naseberry – known as sapodilla in other Caribbean islands, but in Cuba it is often called Mamee Sapote, though it is not related to the Mammee. This tropical fruit is about 3 inches in diameter with rough brown skin and a sweet brownish-purple pulp. It has a taste similar to toffee.

Oregano (*Origanum vulgare*) – a popular herb in Cuban cooking and native to Europe. The species grown in Cuba has a fleshier leaf and grows abundantly in the rich red soil of the huertas.

Pak choi – this is now grown extensively in Cuba especially in urban gardens. You will see it in most of the markets.

Papaya – called fruta bomba in Cuba. Large cylindrical melon-like fruit of a tree native to the Caribbean. The orange-yellow skin is thin and smooth and, when ripe, the flesh is quite sweet with a musty taste. Usually eaten raw with a squeeze of lime.

Paprika – a spice made from the grinding of dried sweet red peppers. This seasoning was brought to Cuba by the Spanish and is used to season and colour many dishes, as well as for making sausages.

Peppers – cubans use a lot of sweet peppers in their cooking but traditionally they do not like the use of hot peppers. However, with the development of Nuevo Latino cuisine, hot peppers such as Scotch Bonnet are making their way into the kitchen.

Pimientos – also called allspice, these are the dark brown berries of an evergreen tree native to the Caribbean. They resemble large peppercorns and their flavour is reminiscent of a blend of cloves, cinnamon and nutmeg.

Plantain – a greenish to yellow or black banana-shaped fruit (the shade of colour depends on the stage of ripening) of a large shrub called *Musa paradisiacal*. It is also called platano. When not ripe, it is hard and contains loads of starch. Its skin remains green and has a neutral taste. If kept at room temperature for about a week, it gradually goes through different phase of ripeness. When the skin is light yellow, it is half ripe and assumes a sweet taste if eaten at this stage. If left for a couple more days, it would become very ripe, with the skin becoming black and the fruit soft. The starch would have changed into sucrose. This nutritious fruit can be eaten boiled whether green, yellow or black. It can be fried. When still green and fried, it is called plantain chips. If yellow or black and fried, it is referred to as banana chips. It can be mashed and used to thicken soup, or even eaten like mashed potatoes.

Sofrito – this term literally means lightly fried and describes a sauce that is the foundation of many Cuban dishes. Made with either onions or garlic, or both, it contains tomatoes, peppers, herbs, spices and sometimes ham.

Sugar and sugar cane – an ingredient that changed the course of Cuban history when it was brought to the island to be harvested for rum. The sugar and juice is extracted by crushing the stems. Apart from sugar and the delicious sugar cane juice called guarapo, other byproducts include molasses, from which rum is made.

Sweet potato – called boniato in Cuba. This edible tuber is grown throughout the tropics and is a staple of the Cuban diet. The skin varies from brown to deep pink to white and the flesh also varies from orange to white.

Rice – the Cubans eat rice with every meal. In fact it is well known that a Cuban doesn't feel as if he has eaten a proper meal unless there is rice on the plate, usually accompanied by black beans.

Romeo y Juliet – the combination of guava paste and fresh cheese is referred to as Romeo y Juliet. It is popular as a dessert or as a breakfast treat, spread on, or served hot with cheese inside an empanada pastry, as a kind of miniature pie.

Saffron – the world's most expensive spice is derived from the saffron crocus. The stigmas, style and stalk are dried and either left whole or ground to a powder, which is used to both flavour and give dishes a rich golden red colour. It is used when making paellas, which the Cubans have inherited from their Spanish ancestors.

Salsa – means sauce and can refer to any sauce, whereas salsa cruda is a raw sauce.

Sour oranges – also called Seville, bitter and Valencia oranges. Originally from Spain, the flesh of the sour orange is too sour to eat but is used extensively in Cuban dishes to season and to make Mojo.

Tapioca – a flavourless, starchy ingredient, or fecula, produced from treated and dried yuca (cassava) root and used in cooking. It is similar to sago and is commonly used to make a milk pudding similar to rice pudding.

Tapioca flour – also called tapioca starch, this is a refined white flour made from the yuca (cassava) root. Gluten-free, it is mainly used as a thickener for sauces, soups and stews but it can also be used in baking.

Thyme – one of the most prolific herbs of the Caribbean, found growing on most islands. In Cuba it is used to season many savoury dishes. When combined with oregano and cumin it makes a delicious seasoning for pork.

Vanilla – a popular flavouring in Cuba for drinks and desserts.

Yuca/cassava – a plant belonging to the spurge family. Native to South America, it is now widely grown throughout the tropics for its starch-containing roots, from which tapioca and bread are made. The edible parts are the tuberous root and leaves. Nutritionally, cassava is comparable to potatoes, but with twice the fibre content and a higher level of potassium.

INDEX